WordPress

Ultimate Beginner's Guide to Creating Your Own Website or Blog

Andrew Mckinnon

without the consent of the author or copyright owner. Legal action will be pursued if this is breached.

<u>Disclaimer Notice:</u>

Please note the information contained within this document is for educational and entertainment purposes only. Every attempt has been made to provide accurate, up-to-date and reliable complete information. No warranties of any kind are expressed or implied. Readers acknowledge that the author is not engaging in the rendering of legal, financial, medical, or professional advice.

By reading this document, the reader agrees that under no circumstances are we responsible for any losses, direct or indirect, which are incurred as a result of the use of information contained within this document, including, but not limited to, errors, omissions, or inaccuracies.

Other Best-Selling books by Andrew McKinnon on Amazon.com

Amazon Echo: Master Your Amazon Echo; User Guide and Manual

#1 Best-Seller

Amazon Echo is the future. It allows you to control almost anything via your voice. Andrew McKinnon has been given a prototype before it came out and has had more time than anyone to review it and present a great user guide. Show off to your friends how technologically advanced you are. The Amazon Echo will allow you to control everything you want by your own command. Never have to get up again without the Echo; it is truly the power of your voice. Be a part of the future!

Check it out! ---- http://amzn.to/1G3FNe2

YouTube: Ultimate YouTube Guide to Building a Channel, Audience and to Start Making Passive Income

#1 Best Seller

YouTube may be the most visited website on the web for the majority of people. Thousands start new channels every day with the hope of gaining a large audience and subscribers — some do make it, but the odds are slim. This best-seller will give you the keys to unlock passive income from YouTube and build a massive channel in the niche of your choosing!

Check it out! ---- http://amzn.to/1gk75bl

Photoshop: Master Photoshop Through Proven Tips, Tricks and Strategies

Have you ever wanted to learn how to edit like a professional but never wanted to take hours of schooling? If so, this is the book for you! Andrew McKinnon has broken down the "hard" process of learning Photoshop. You will become truly skilled. He shows you, in easy terms, what many call hard strategies to learn. After reading this book, you will fully understand Photoshop!

Check it out! ---- http://amzn.to/1HJ2ZDI

Apple Watch: Master Your Apple Watch - Complete User Guide from Beginners to Expert

With ***Apple Watch: Master Your Apple Watch - Complete User Guide from Beginners to Expert***, you'll learn how to control media remotely from your Apple Watch. This book also explains how to use this device with Apple Pay and Passbook for more everyday convenience. You can also stay healthy and fit with essential exercising tips for the Apple Watch!

Check it out! ---- http://amzn.to/1QcFsg0

--

Hacking: Ultimate Hacking for Beginners, How to Hack

#1 Best-Seller

This book will give you the tools to understand hacking — many reviewers called it Amazon's best book on hacking in 2015. This book will give you the tools to fully understand what hacking is and how to do it. This is especially important to know in today's society, as it is happening all the time. Read this book and become knowledgeable in the art of hacking!

Check it out! ---- http://amzn.to/1S47Qks

Table of Contents

Introduction

WordPress is becoming extremely popular among a lot of people who want to create their own website but don't really have the skills or expertise necessary to create code and develop the site entirely on their own. It's a free service, although there are several options that will allow you to upgrade your usage for a fee. What's great about WordPress however, is the versatility and the ability to personalize everything.

Throughout this book, we'll talk about some of the best ways that you can use WordPress to develop your own website, and how you can use that website as your own personal blog and gain more readers. After all, the point of having a website is so that people can come visit it, right? Well that's what we believe the purpose is, and that means we're going to help you achieve that particular purpose by walking you through the steps you need to get started.

WordPress is actually one of the easier methods of creating a website and that's why it's growing faster than most others. So don't just sit back and let everyone else pass you by. Jump to the front of the line and start making some changes that are going to improve your life (and possibly the lives of others). Start sharing your knowledge with the help of a WordPress website or blog. It's easier than you might think and it's going to give you a great website by the time you're all done building.

Chapter 1

What Is WordPress?

The first thing you need to understand is what WordPress really is. Well, it's actually CMS software. That means that it's code that allows you to create your own website and web pages. The software takes care of all the coding for you (like where the text should be and what colors you choose for text or backgrounds). Not that long ago, if you wanted a website, you had to handwrite all the code for it. When you looked at that code it generally looked like a pretty jumbled mess. But all that has changed recently.

Software programs like WordPress have been invented to take the difficulty out of the process. This means that you no longer have to handwrite every piece of information. On WordPress, you use a page that looks very similar to Microsoft Word to write out your posts. That means you don't have to figure out the code for italics, bold, underline, size increase or anything else. Instead, you just change the size, underline, italicize, or bold any of the text that you want and make it look the way you like. WordPress will do the rest.

CMS means "content management system," so your content is being taken care of by the system. Now, it's not going to produce anything that you don't tell it to. You need to make sure that you develop your website so it's beneficial to your overall success, by making it look good to all of your potential readers and viewers. However, WordPress comes with some functions that will make this entire process a lot easier to understand and use at the same time.

Why Use WordPress?

Very often, beginners want to know why they should switch from their old site to WordPress. What has it got that their existing platform hasn't? Many people make the mistake of thinking of WordPress as nothing more than a blogger's platform and, although that's what it started out as, it's no longer the case. WordPress has evolved though the years to become one of the most versatile content management systems in the world. Yes, you can still use WordPress to create your blog, but you can also create websites that are fully functioning, along with mobile applications.

The best thing about WordPress is that it is highly flexible and very easy to use, and those are the two main reasons why WordPress has become more popular. According to recent research, it is now responsible for powering almost 25% of all websites on the net today.

So, let's have a look at the best reasons why you should use WordPress today to create your blog or website:

1. It's Free

WordPress is completely free to download, install, and use, as well as to modify. It can be used for any type of website and is open source — this means that the source code is free for anyone to look into, study, and modify for their own use.

Right now, there are more than 2600 different themes, and more than 30,000 different free plugins, all of which can be downloaded and used on any website. To run WordPress all you need is a computer, access to the Internet, a domain name, and a web host (depending on which version of WordPress you use — more about that in a bit).

The nature of open source software lends itself to being community software, which means that WordPress is maintained by a group of volunteers. Most of these are consultants for WordPress; that is, people who have an active interest in seeing it grow and evolve even further. Any person can make a contribution to WordPress — writing patches, plugins, creating a theme, helping to answer support questions, updating documentation and translating WordPress for other users.

When you opt to download and use WordPress, you will become a part of that huge community, and will be eligible for free support from other members, to download free themes, plugins and, when you have gained some experience, to give something back to the community.

2. It Is Easy to Use and to Learn

Millions of people use WordPress on a daily basis, and new people are entering the community every day when they make their very first website powered by WordPress. The biggest reason why people choose WordPress is that it is so easy to learn and is very easy to use.

There are plenty of how-to guides, detailed articles and explanations, as well as a support system that helps newbies to the community get set up and learn their way around. These are there for you to use, written and provided by people who have been in the same situation as you, so make use of them.

3. It Is Extendable with Themes and Plugins

Most people who use WordPress are in no way experienced programmers or web designers. In fact, most people who start using it have no experience or even knowledge of designing a website.

So, why is it so popular? Simply because it contains many thousands of different templates, many of them free, that you can choose from, to give your website the kind of look you want, without the expense or work of a web designer. To be fair, no matter what the subject of your website, there will be a theme that will match it, whether it's photography, pets, vintage cars, or whatever you choose to base your site on.

Not only that, you can easily customize any WordPress theme to suit what you want because most come with an options panel — you can change the color scheme, upload a new logo, change the background for something more suitable, make sliders, and do lots of other cool and fun things to give your website the personal touch. And you get all of this without writing one single piece of code!

WordPress is also highly flexible, and plugins can be used to extend it. Similar to themes, there are thousands of plugins, free and premium, that you can use to add extra functionality to your WordPress site.

4. It Is Search Engine-Friendly

Because it is written with standard-compliant, high-quality code, and it produces semantic markups, it is very friendly when it comes to search engines. WordPress is what we call SEO-friendly, and it can be made even more so if you choose to use the SEO plugin.

5. It Is Easy to Manage

WordPress has an updater built in to it that lets you update plugins and themes from your admin dashboard. It will also tell you when WordPress itself is ready for an update to a new version so you can stay up to date with a simple click of a button. You can also set up regular automated backups to keep your content safe.

6. It Is Safe and Secure

WordPress was developed with safety and security in mind, so it is perfectly safe to run any website from. However, the number of threats on the Internet is growing by the year and there are always attackers waiting in the wings. You should always make sure you have your own virus checker and anti-malware programs installed as an extra layer of security and protection.

7. It is Able to Handle a Number of Different Media Types

When you use WordPress, you don't have to stick to just using text, as it comes with the ability and support required to handle other media types, including audio, images and videos. It also supports oEmbed-enabled websites, so you can easily embed photos from Instagram, videos from YouTube, tweets and audio from SoundCloud just by pasting the URL of the relevant one into the post you are writing. You can also choose to allow visitors to your site to embed videos in their comments to you.

How Can I Use WordPress?

There are lots of ways that WordPress can be used; it is one of the most open programs ever. You can use WordPress in the following ways:

- As an arcade

- As a blog

- As a content management system

- As a gallery

- As a portfolio

- As a rating website

- As a shopping store

- As a video or movie collection site

- As a membership site

Which Version of WordPress Do I Need?

That depends entirely on what you are intending to do. Not many people realize that there are actually two versions of WordPress and, of those that do, many are still confused about the difference between them.

In simple terms, WordPress.org is used as a repository for information and software grabbing, while WordPress.com focuses on providing hosting services. Now, let's look at each one in a little more depth:

WordPress.org

This where WordPress is free to the public, along with thousands of different plugins, many free and some premium, that you can buy separately. This is the best place for those who want to get started on their first website, or those who are happy with the DIY solution, and it provides access to support forums and loads of "how to" guides and information. You can modify your site design and add functionality, going as far as your creative side will allow you to.

Here you will also find all the documentation you need on how to install WordPress, walkthroughs of your very first post, how to choose categories and so much more. And, considering it is all free, the documentation is exceptionally well written and very helpful.

On WordPress.org, you get WP Codex, allowing you to locate everything you need to get WordPress up and running on your own domain. And to make things even easier, most web hosts include a "one-click" WordPress installation script.

So, with WordPress.org, the only limits are you and your creativity. You don't need to pay any money to get rid of third-party ads and, as there are no restrictions, you can go as far as you like in modifying the core PHP, add in some fancy jQuery elements and use whatever theme or plugin you want.

One thing is missing, though. Although the setup is easy with one-click installation, you do need to get your own web host, and they are not free. Costs do vary from host to host, but for a good one, on a typical small or medium site, you can expect to pay up to about $15 a month. Later on, I will talk more about hosts, how to find the right one and give you a few options to choose from. You will also have to pay to renew your domain name every year, although that doesn't cost a great deal.

WordPress.com

Things are somewhat different on WordPress.com. Installing WordPress is dead simple and you get web hosting included, usually for free. Obviously, the pros of this are pretty clear. As well as getting a good quality web host, you also get built-in spam protection, automatic updates, automatic backups, security, a plugins and other services that are not available elsewhere, or at least not to start with.

So, that's the good news. The downside of all this is that you will not be able to modify the core PHP source code and, let's be honest here, even those that are new to WordPress often find that they want to make the odd change here and there. You also can't upload plugins, although you can use those that are in WordPress, but you will only get access to a tiny fraction of the 19,000 or so that are available on the other site.

And, while you have around 200 different themes to choose from, you can't upload your own one; you also can't make too many changes to those that you can access.

Now, should you wish to take things further, you can pay money if you want:

• Remove third-party ads from your site for $30 per year.

• Buy a custom design package that will give you some control, although not a lot, over customizing the theme and making a few basic CSS changes (still no PHP or FTP) for $30 per year.

• Buy extra storage, starting from $20 per year.

- Buy VideoPress for $60 per year so you can roll out your own videos, although you can embed YouTube videos without that.

- Premium themes will cost you between $45 and $100 each and they cannot be taken with you if you choose to go self-hosted later on down the line.

Which Is Better?

Cost should never be one of the main factors in your choice, although, to be fair, you do only get what you pay for. At some point, no matter which one you choose, you are going to have to pay something, so base your choice on what you really want to do. That is the deciding factor here. This is your website, or blog, that you are building, your brand and your voice. How you chose to present yourself will have a direct bearing on the choice of site you make.

WordPress.com hosting can give you a cheap way of sharing yourself with others. You don't need to pay for the extras if you don't need them; much will depend on the type of site you are building. A home or personal site can be done for next to nothing.

A professional site, on the other hand, is a different matter. For this, you will want to have complete control over your web hosting, your branding, advertising, and more besides. You will want your website to look fantastic, you'll want the right theme and the right plugins and you will need to be able to, or at least know someone else who can, get into FTP and PHP, and everything else that will make your site the success you want it to be.

And, if you have already gone with WordPress.com and set up your site, you can migrate over at any time you choose — you will just need to find the right hosting company.

Chapter 2
Choosing a Host

Once you've decided to use WordPress you need to make sure that you choose a host for your website. As we mentioned, WordPress is a software system and that means it needs to operate somewhere. You need to have a website host where it can use its software. You can choose to work directly with WordPress and create your website on their host site (this is free for the basic package), or you can choose to work with a more advanced website host. The important thing to keep in mind is your end goals and what you want out of the project.

WordPress as a website is not bad. It is going to provide you with everything you need, or want, in a host when you're first starting out. If you're looking to create your blog just for yourself, this may be a great way to do it. On the other hand, if you're looking to create a blog that other people can use, one that will be easy to locate and access, you want to use a good host that's going to be easy to find, and that's going to allow you to create your own website address.

Think about the websites that you go to most frequently. How long is the web address? Most likely it isn't very long. Like Facebook.com or Google.com. These are very short. What you want in your website address is also something short. The longer it is, the more difficult it is to remember, and the less it has to do with you or your actual topic the harder it is to remember as well. Unfortunately, if you work with WordPress as your website host you need to include WordPress in part of your website title (unless you choose a higher level, paid package). This makes it harder for people to find you, and they aren't as likely to take you seriously.

Now, you can purchase your website name (called your domain). You can do this through WordPress or through a variety of other websites as well. Your domain name is the address that people use to find you. If you make it simple and catchy you're likely to draw more people in. But make it too long and complicated and you'll drive them away simply because they can't remember what your address was when they want it.

Another thing you need to consider is the advertising that's going to be on your web page. If you choose a free web host, you're likely going to get a lot of ads on your website, and you aren't going to get any benefits from them. Unlike some programs like Google AdSense that allow you to get revenue by posting ads, these ads provide revenue for the host that you're using. Your website gets clogged up (potentially turning away some of your users) and you don't get anything out of it.

You don't want to have advertisements or banners on your website unless you're making some money off them, so look for hosts that don't have these things. If you're looking for a free host, you'll have to work with them and make the best of it. If you're looking for something high-quality, however, be willing to pay a little bit more money just to get rid of all those ads, and make sure that your readers are going to have an easy to use and readable platform.

Look at how much web space you'll get. Any host will tell you how much space your website can have for the fee that you're going to pay. This is something you'll pay more for, because the more space you want the more your host is going to charge you. You may look at what's available and think some of the sizes are extremely large and that you could never use up all that space. Chances are you would be right. Even a reasonably advanced website with some pictures, videos, sound clips and more is only going to be about 5 MB in total.

If you're going to include a lot of different sound, video, and pictures on your website, you can upgrade your size a bit to make sure that you'll have enough room. The last thing you want is to create your website and then find out that some of your files don't load because your web host limited what could be used. It's better to aim a little high than to aim low, but don't pay a fortune for astronomical amounts of space. You're never going to need a gigabyte of space for one website, for example.

Look at the size your files can be when uploading to your website. Different hosts may put different limits, such as 400 KB per file. You want to make sure that the limits will be large enough for anything you want to put up. The same goes for different file types. Make sure any file types you may want to use (such as PDF, JPG, etc.) are all accepted by the web host. Not all hosts will do this, and that means you might have a great file and not be able to use it.

The reliability and the speed at which your website loads are also extremely important. If your host doesn't give you a reliable connection, then your readers are going to go somewhere else. They don't want to spend a lot of time trying to find you when the site goes down again. They're going to look somewhere else to get what they need a lot more reliably. They're also going to look around for fast speeds. You want to make sure that your website can be fully retrieved quickly and that depends on your host, as well.

Bandwidth is also extremely important. You need to make sure that your website can get plenty of traffic throughout the entire month, and whenever someone wants it. Bandwidth basically measures how many people can visit your website in a given month. If your bandwidth is small, no one will be able to find your website for the rest of the month when it's used up. You want to have at least 1-3 GB of bandwidth allowed per month to ensure that your website is going to remain up all month. If you continue to increase your monthly viewers, however, you may need to increase this slightly more.

If you use up your bandwidth, then your host may cut you off. That means they pull your website off their server until you pay a bill, or reach a new month and get renewed. You never want that to happen and that's why it's so crucial to make sure that you pay what it takes to get a decent bandwidth. If you're less than 1 GB, you're not going to make it through the month once people start finding out about your website, and that means you're going to lose readers.

Make sure you can use an SSL (secure server) if you're going to be selling anything to your readers. If you decide that you want to sell something you want your website to be secure because you're accepting credit card information and payments. You want to protect your readers and buyers and they want to make sure they're going to be safe as well. You're a lot less likely to actually get the sales that you want if you don't have an SSL connection, but not all hosts are going to allow this. Make sure that yours will.

Finally, check out the type of technical support you're going to get. Especially when you're paying for a service, you want to make sure that you can get assistance at any time if you need it. That means day or night, weekday or weekend, you want to be able to get in touch with someone to find out what's wrong with your website or what you need to do to fix a problem. If you don't have technical support 24/7, it could result in people not being able to access the information they want, or need, on your website and they may go elsewhere.

How to Make Sure You Get the Best WordPress Web Hosting

Web hosting is one of the most important aspects to a successful website; after all, your site won't be visible on the Internet without it. Yet it is the single most overlooked component. It can be a bit of a minefield choosing from all the web hosting services available, but getting the right one is part of the equation in ensuring that your site is a success. There are lots of different types of hosting options available for WordPress, including Shared, Free, Dedicated, VPS, and Managed. For this part of the chapter, I am going to tell you what is required for hosting a WordPress site, the things you need to consider when choosing, and then a few recommendations for the top WordPress hosting sites.

WordPress Hosting Requirements

You might be surprised to learn that WordPress is actually a very lightweight script, and is fully compatible with virtually all of the best hosting companies. WordPress has very few requirements, the main one being that the web host is running PHP 5.2.4 or later. Because WordPress is so popular now, most of the top hosting companies have one-click install for it, making it dead simple to use. All of the web hosts I will tell you about later offer a full support service for WordPress sites.

What to Consider When You Choose Your WordPress Web Host

Obviously, the top factors that you need to consider are speed, reliability and security, but the single most important thing to consider is you, what your needs are for your website. Thinking about your needs before you buy a WordPress hosting service can save you a small fortune.

Your Needs

There are lots of different types of hosting available as I mentioned above, so let's have a look at what each option offers in terms of your needs:

Free

Free webhosting is available for WordPress, but most of the sites that offer it have some kind of catch. If you look at small groups, or online forums, you'll find the free options, most of which are managed by an individual who is looking to recover a bit of revenue by reselling part of their server space. Some of them might ask that you add a text link in the footer of your site, or others will request specifically that you have to have their banner ads in view on your website. They cover the cost of you not paying for their server space by selling the banner ad, or the text link, and they pocket any profit as well.

One of the biggest downsides to taking up free hosting is that, ads aside, they are not particularly reliable. You don't know when the service might suddenly stop, and you can be left in the lurch without a minute's notice.

Takeaway — If your website is more serious than just something for fun, avoid free hosting options.

Shared

This is, by a long shot, the most popular form of WordPress hosting used by newbies. It is affordable and it is a great starting point. In shared hosting, large servers are shared among lots of sites. By having a lot of different sites on the same server, providers can offer you their server at a better rate. There is one catch, though, and you see it with most providers that offer shared hosting: They always say there are unlimited resources. This simply isn't true because there is no such thing. You will still be bound by usage restrictions, and if your website grows enough to start taking up more space on the server, you will be, very politely, forced to upgrade. If they don't do this, it will have a bad effect on the performance that other hosted sites see. Look at this way — the more your business grows, the bigger your overheads are going to be, so be prepared to pay for success.

Takeaway — The best solution for those who are starting out in the blogging business and for small businesses.

VPS

Virtual private server (VPS) hosting refers to having a VM, or virtual machine. It is a way of splitting a physical server into a lot of different ones, taking into account the needs of the individual customer. Although you will still be sharing the server with others, you do have pretty much the same control as you would with a dedicated server. This hosting method also boasts the convenience of a physical computer that can be configured to run various types of server software. This kind of hosting is often used by medium-sized businesses or bloggers, developers, and intermediate users to start scaling up their business. If you have no technical knowledge, then opt for a managed VPS. This means that the host will provide and manage system upgrades and are there if you need any help.

Takeaway — Good for high-traffic websites and blogs, medium-sized businesses, and developers and designers just starting out.

Dedicated

A dedicated server is a physical server that you lease from the hosting provider, giving you complete control over the server. This means you get to choose the hardware, the operating system, and all sorts of other options. If you are just beginning, you really don't need a dedicated server and, if you do opt for this, but have no experience with a server, or don't have a systems administrator, choose a managed dedicated server. Most of these employ system administrators on a full-time basis that offer support and server monitoring. They are also responsible for software updates. Really and truthfully, you don't need a dedicated server until your website is receiving a fair-sized, steady stream of traffic.

Takeaway — Ideal for blogs and websites that have a high stream of traffic.

Managed

Because there are so many users of WordPress now, not many hosting sites offer managed hosting. If you take an account with a managed provider, you can only host a WordPress site, nothing else. The benefit of this is that they do everything. They will optimize your website's performance, make sure that it is secure, and create regular backups for you. They will also tell you if a plugin you are using is not doing your site any good.

Managed hosting is fast and it is hassle-free, with lots of good quality support from those who have a lot of experience with WordPress. This might sound great but the plan options you get to choose from are not cheap. The cheapest one, a personal account that allows you to host one site with a maximum of 25,000 visitors per month, will cost you around $30 per month. The next on up allows you multiple sites, but it will cost you around $100 per month, not something a new blogger can afford to pay.

Takeaway - Hassle-free and fast but not cheap; ideal for experienced bloggers or businesses that can justify the expenditure.

So now that you know what your options are, it's time to make up your mind! Each of the following web hosting sites offer full WordPress support, including one-click installation, but do bear in mind these are not the only ones; there are others, so do your homework thoroughly before you make your choice:

Blue Host

Started in 1996, this is one of the longest running web host companies, as well as being one of the most popular and largest brands when it comes to WordPress. They are an officially recommended WordPress hosting company as well. You will never have a slow website, even with a lot of traffic, and they offer a free domain and free software to build your website with, including loads of templates. They also do good deals for WordPress newbies.

InMotion

A well-known brand, especially for business sites, and offering very reliable performance. They provide award-winning support and guarantee uptime of 99.9%, making them one of the favorites. Their support is unmatched, especially in the U.S., and they are always on hand to help.

Their hosting is optimized for active bloggers and it offers good options for growing your site.

Web Hosting Hub

This is the easiest way for a small business to get a presence online. It offers a very easy-to-use control panel, a website builder, and amazingly good support. It also offers good value for the price, and you will find it hard to beat their price. They also give discounts to WordPress beginners.

HostGator

This is most likely the one you have heard of and hosts more than 8 million different domains. They offer one-click, 99.9% uptime, and support 24/7, making them one of the easiest choices for web hosting.

SiteGround

One of the most popular of all the WordPress hosting sites, they are well recognized within the community. They offer a unique solution, including security and speed solutions in-house, 24/7 support, automatic updates, CDN, on-click staging, WordPress caching and GIT version control. They offer location-specific hosting, having data centers in Singapore, the U.S. and Europe.

Chapter 3
Installing WordPress Locally on Your Computer

Usually, WordPress is automatically downloaded with the help of the web hosting service you have chosen. Most web hosts need you to download WordPress and follow their instructions; it is a hassle-free, easy way (for those without the technical knowledge required) to install and start using WordPress. But the disadvantage of using WordPress via a web host is that as soon as you hit "Publish," the entire website goes live for the world to see. As great as that may sound, you will not be able to try out tests on new themes, styles, or backgrounds without it affecting the actual website. When you are a beginner to blogging or creating webpages with WordPress, this should not affect you as much. It is only when you start getting proficient and want to try out effective themes that this will turn into a problem.

The problem with tweaking live sites is that when you change the theme, WordPress may crash and bring your entire website down until you fix it. When you are a beginner, fixing it yourself will take quite some research. When you do not have a backup, getting the website back to how it was will be an arduous job. Imagine spending all the time you put from the beginning all over again, just to get back what you lose. Of course, your WordPress crashing can also be because your hosting service went down. It is therefore important to use a well-trusted hosting service.

If WordPress is installed locally on your computer (called localhost) you can create, edit, test, and try out everything available without it affecting the website. Your live website will be untouched, while you play around with the formatting options and such to give a personal touch. Also, with zero risk, you will be more motivated to try out new plug-ins and themes. You don't even need a maintenance plug-in to pull your website out of service for a long time so you can add a few changes. And the best part is that you can work offline! Imagine a workspace where you have no distractions like social media to coax you into procrastinating and putting off your next blog or update. You can of course, update your live website to include all the changes you have made in your offline website.

Other than just testing new plugins, you can also check their compatibility with other plugins or with the theme itself. Plugins are usually designed to work perfectly with all themes, but some of them are coded by beginners without much experience. They may crash when activated alongside other plugins or when used with a particular theme. When they do crash, bringing up your website is going to take quite some time (not to mention quite some effort as well) and, in the worst-case scenario, you might need to make use of a backup. For these reasons, having a localhost is beneficial, because you can figure out what went awry without having to bring your website down.

To download WordPress, you need to have a software stack for web servers like WAMP and XAMPP. These are both software stacks that contain MySQL database, PHP, and OpenSSL. WAMP (acronym for Windows, Apache, MySQL, and PHP) can be used only in Windows. XAMPP denotes the same, but the X stands for any operating system, meaning it is compatible with Windows, Linux, or OS X. If you own a Windows computer, WAMP is definitely the best choice for you. As with most Windows software, WAMP comes with a huge variety of features, and the best part is, *it's completely free!* Follow these steps to download WordPress locally with the help of WAMP:

1)   Go to www.wampserver.com and download either the 32- or 64-bit version, depending on your computer's configurations.

2)   Open the executable file and follow the on-screen instructions to install WAMP. When prompted to choose your default web browser, you can select anything you want.

3)   Launch WAMP once it's installed (it should be visible in your task bar). You now have to create a database for your WordPress. Do not fret! It is very easy if you follow the next step.

4)   Click on the *WAMP* icon in your task bar and select "phpMyAdmin." Click on "Databases" in the new browser, and then "Create" to create your database. You can name your database as you wish. And voila! Your database is now created.

5)   Head over to WordPress.com and download their latest stable version. It will be a zip folder, so extract it to

c:\wamp\www. It is important to copy the files here and not anywhere else.

6)   Now there are two ways you can accomplish the next task. You can rename the "wp-config-sample.php" to "wp-config.php" and change your database name, while keeping username as "root" and password as a blank. This is manual configuration. You can also go to http://localhost/wordpress/ and let WordPress will guide you through the same procedure after you click on "Create a Configuration File."

7)   Now just install WordPress after filling out the form. The form will ask you for a website title, your personal username, password, and of course, your e-mail.

With this, WordPress has been locally installed on your computer with WAMP, and you can start using it to test different themes and plug-ins without affecting your live website.

WAMP is a great software bundle, but it does have some issues. For one, it is compatible only with Windows. If you own a Linux or OS X machine, you will not be able to use WAMP. This is why XAMPP is slightly better, as it's a cross-platform web server environment. To install WordPress using XAMPP follow these steps:

1)   Head over to www.apachefriends.org and install their XAMPP package for your corresponding operating system.

2)   Open the file, and proceed with the installation process. When you are asked to select the required components, it is enough if you check MySQL and phpMyAdmin, as the others aren't really necessary for WordPress.

3)   Proceed with installation, and uncheck the box when Bitnami is prompted.

4)   XAMPP is finally installed!

5)   Now open the XAMPP Control Panel from the folder you had selected, and start MySQL and Apache.

6)   As with WAMP, you need a database for your WordPress. In the MySQL service, click on *Admin* button. Create a database with a name of your choice.

7)   Now, install WordPress from WordPress.org.

8)   This step is important. Extract the WordPress folder to the "htdocs" folder in your XAMPP directory.

9)   Now you need to create a configuration file. Follow the same steps as mentioned in the WAMP section.

10)   Go to http://localhost/wordpress and follow the same procedure as above to get your WordPress up and running offline!

When you want to change themes on a live website, you have to pull the website down, then either reset your MySQL database, or re-install WordPress (which is several times easier). If you decide to re-install WordPress, make sure you create a backup of all your themes and database just in case you need them back. If you are experienced enough, this won't seem like a bother, but when you just start out, it helps enormously to just try and customize your website's theme with WordPress installed locally.

Installing WordPress locally is not as difficult as one would assume it to be. It may seem impossible when you first start out because you will not understand most of the jargon involved but, as you become proficient with WordPress, installing it locally is one of the best professional choices you can make.

Chapter 4
Design Your Site

Now that you have a host, it's time start designing the actual website. This is the fun part because you get to let your own creativity really shine and start to express yourself. You want to make sure that your website is going to represent you, after all. You are the unique part of your website because you're the one with the information and the knowledge to share. By expressing yourself, you're also helping to express that information.

Think about what your topic will be while you're designing. This will also play a role in what type of designs you use. For example, if you're writing a website about hunting, you're probably not going to fill it with background images of pink and butterflies. The two just don't match and people are less likely to take you as a serious hunter if you have all those butterflies (even though you may be the best hunter there is anywhere, it's just not going to happen). So make your design match (or somewhat match) what you're going for.

Your design or background starts with your theme through WordPress. If you choose a free account, you will be given a limited number of "themes" to choose from. These will show how your website is formatted, as well as some of the backgrounds you are able to use. Some are created by users and some are created by WordPress itself. You get to choose a theme that you want to work with so you don't have to customize quite as much. The software will customize your information and background to give you a basis for your work rather than just a blank page that you have to add everything to.

If you decide to upgrade to a paid account, you will also be able to use a variety of additional themes that are generally more complex and more detailed as well. Or you can create your own theme with the assistance of WordPress. Once you choose a theme, you can customize it and work on ways to make it truly unique for your own website. You can continue working with the design and make changes to much of it.

If we stick with the hunting example, you don't have to design your entire website in camouflage. You could choose a solid color like black, blue, green, or brown. You may choose a pattern like leopard spots or feathers. These things have to do with your theme and they are going to make you seem a little more serious to the people that are actually reading your website. Of course, the background that you choose is not the only thing that you will need to have on your website. There's a lot more involved than that.

The next thing to look at is your font. You want to make sure that you're consistent throughout your entire website with the type of font you use. Things like titles and headings, or even your website name, can be in a different font. You can actually use different fonts for each of these if you choose. But make sure that they match. What that means is all your titles should have the same font and all of your headings should have the same font. The same font means the same style and the same size. It doesn't always have to be the same color, depending on the information you're writing, but the rest should be consistent.

Your normal text should always be the same. It should always be the same font style and the same size, but it can also change color depending on different aspects. In general, you'll want all of your fonts (no matter what they're for) to be a dark color so it is easy to read. Now, if you choose a dark background, this is generally reversed; that is, you want your font to be a light color. You don't ever want your reader to have to struggle to read what you've written. That applies to color, style, and size of your font.

The reason for all of this is consistency. People in general like consistency. When your titles all look different, it seems sloppy, as though you don't really know what you're doing, and that makes people less likely to rely on you. When your information is difficult to read, this also makes it more difficult for people to stay with your website. They may like the information and may think you're very smart, but no one wants to spend all their time struggling through one article when they could have read an entire other website.

Once you've settled on what you want for your background and your text, you need to think about the organization. You want to have more than one page, so your readers can get different types of information. You also want to make sure that you have different areas for things like blog posts and images. If we continue to stick with the example of the hunting website you might want a page for your blog, a pictures page, a news page, and maybe a forum. These types of pages will work in a lot of different topic areas, actually.

Blog — The blog section is where you will write your personal information. In the hunting website example, you might write about hunting trips you go on, products that you've tried and liked, various animals that you've hunted or would hunt, etc. This is where you put down all your personal experiences, and the things that you would talk about to a friend. You might even give advice, or let people in on things they might not know about hunting, specific animals, locations, or even weapons.

Pictures — On this page you can post pictures of trophies you've bagged and you can invite your readers to share some information as well. You could also post pictures of places that you've been, things you've done, experiences you've had, or anything else. Share pictures of your topic and you engaging in your topic. Invite your readers to share some pictures of themselves doing the same. This is going to encourage more people, and it's going to keep them interested in the topic even more as well because they can see what other people got from it.

News — This page is possibly one of the most important. This is where people are going to get more information, not only about your website, but about the world as well. You want your news to be focused on your topic area, but you want it to be extensive as well. So, if laws are changing in one particular state, you want to write about it. Share this type of information with your readers so they know what's going on around the country and around the world as well. This will help them know what they can and can't do and it will also help them recognize your site as the place to go if they ever need more information.

Forum — This is another great page to have because it's going to help you share information with your readers and find out what they know or want to know, as well. You can start out by having a forum with questions, or information you've created, and then open it up to readers so they can comment, or answer/ask questions. After that, you may want to open it further so that your readers can create their own posts, and their own forum questions. That's how you can find out what they want to know about, and you can create blog posts geared towards that information.

Creating pages is actually very simple to do on WordPress. All you need to do is tell the software that you want a new page and it will create that page for you. Then you go customize any additional information, such as where the text is going to go on the page, what the background is going to look like, and where pictures are going to be placed. You can also choose to keep all of these things static, so they automatically appear the same on every webpage that you create for that website. This can be the best move and makes the process easier.

Another thing that you can do with the automation on WordPress is create specific pages. There are specially formatted pages for things like forums, blogs, or a "Contact Us" page. By using the templates, you don't have to spend as much time trying to arrange and organize the page to your liking. There are even different templates within each of these categories, so you can make sure that your website looks exactly the way that you want it to when you're completely done.

Once you've created these pages, you'll be able to create content for them as well. That's what your readers are actually interested in, after all. The design is going to make them enjoy the site, and it's going to make them keep coming back, as well. But what's really going to affect them is how the website looks, and whether they feel as if they can get a lot of information from visiting and reading what you have to say. That's in the next section. But first ...

Top Ten Free WordPress Themes for 2015

The following themes are a tiny sample of what is available, free, in WordPress, and they are merely a representation of what you can expect to find. It is going to be tough to choose the best for your needs, so the ones I have chosen are full of features, flexible, responsive, and multipurpose. They are suitable for any type of business, any size.

1. AccessPress Lite

This is a multipurpose responsive theme aimed at businesses. It has a clean design, a professional look, and loads of really useful features, as well as a great options panel to manage everything. In fact, it offers pretty much what a premium theme would offer, but without the price tag. It is one of the most feature-rich free WordPress themes with loads of useful options, such as:

- Events layout

- Blog layout

- Gallery layout

- Portfolio layout

- Testimonial layout

- Featured posts for home page

- Social media integration

- Quick contact

- Team member layout

- Full width slider

- Multiple home page layout

- Sidebar layout

- Call to action layout

- And loads more besides.

It is compatible with Woo Commerce and bbPress, as well as being translation-ready. Compatible cross-browser, SEO-friendly and it offers RTL support. The theme is translated fully into French, Japanese, Persian, and Danish.

AccessPress Lite is a multipurpose theme and can be used for any type of website, including creative, personal, corporate, travel, photography, portfolio, bloggers, and many more.

2. Pinboard

Pinboard is elegant and is powered by a grid system and advanced theme framework. It has pretty much unlimited options for layouts and styles, perfect for showcasing portfolios or other websites that display multimedia, such as photography, videos, and podcasts.

3. Staple

AccessPress Staple is a very simple and clean theme, responsive and beautifully designed. It features minimal features, but they are highly used features that will help you set your website up quickly and easily. It offers a number of layouts, including:

- Featured posts

- Featured slider

- Boxed

- Full width

- Testimonial

- Blog

- Social media

- Call to action

- And more besides.

It is fully responsive and compatible with both bbPress and Woo Commerce, cross-browser compatible, and translation-ready, as well as being SEO-friendly. It is multipurpose and is deal for any type of business. It has a high compatibility level with many of the most used plugins and offers great customer support.

4. Arcade Basic

Arcade is lightweight and responsive, an HTML5 theme. A theme customizer is included so you can add your own header images, site-width page layout, and much more. Each post on your site can be easily distinguished by using one of the eight supported post formats:

- Video

- Image

- Aside

- Status

- Audio

- Quote

- Link

- Gallery.

Full compatibility with bbPress and BuddyPress and it uses Google Fonts, so it works perfectly on all types of device.

5. Enigma

A multipurpose theme that can be used with any type of site, including blogging. It has cross-browser compatibility and is Retina-ready. Included are four page layouts, two templates, five widgets, the option to add social media links, and a full control panel.

6. GeneratePress

GeneratePress is a very fast and lightweight theme that lets you create a unique website. It has a built-in customizer, and is mobile-responsive, SEO-friendly, cross-browser compatible, and fully compatible with Woo Commerce and BuddyPress. It has eight widget areas, five layouts for the sidebar, five navigation positions, and much more besides.

7. Make

You don't need to touch a single piece of code to build your website using this theme. It is fully flexible and includes loads of customization and a drag-and-drop page builder. You can use this theme to build whatever type of site you want, be it fun- or business-oriented. Start by creating the background, font, logo, and colors that you want, then add and organize your content. Add videos, photos, a gallery, or a slider to any of the pages and make it responsive, so it looks fantastic on any device, be it mobile or desktop. It is fully compatible with Gravity Forms, Woo Commerce, JetPack, Contact Form 7, and WPPageNavi.

8. Root

AccessPress Root is another theme that has a simple design, is clean and responsive, and includes drag-and-drop sections for the home page. It has minimal features, but they are useful to help set up the website, with a wide choice of layouts. It is fully responsive, compatible with bbPress and Woo Commerce, compatible with all browsers, translation-ready, and SEO-friendly, and it offers great support.

9. MH Magazine Lite

This is a free version of a premium theme. It is clean and modern, designed for online magazines, blogs, news websites, and other sites that are editorial related. It offers limited features but good ones — more are available if you buy the full version. It is ideal for someone who doesn't want to make too many changes to start with.

10. AccessPress Parallax

This is a beautiful theme with a parallax design. Because of the 3D effects, it is a popular one for those who want to add a bit of depth to their story. 3D is engaging; it draws in customers and is fun. It is a feature-rich theme, is fully responsive, has an advanced options panel, Google Map integrations, custom logo, and it is SEO-friendly, translation-ready, and so much more besides.

Top Ten Premium WordPress Themes for 2015

Those are the free ones, but what if you want something a bit more, you need a premium them. The following are ten popular premium WordPress themes, each one with its own features, highly customizable and fully adaptable.

1. X - The Theme

This one might have a simple name, but it is packed full of features, just about everything you need. It has multiple designs, which make it ideal for any niche or any purpose. Instead of layout options, you get stacks, which are separate designs. The idea behind it is to make sure that multiple sites don't look too similar. Each installation gives you the option of creating a unique design, thanks largely to the tools available for customization and functions. No coding is needed to customize any aspect, and you can also preview all changes without having to refresh your website. It is fully responsive and ideal for mobile devices and it is used by more than 30,000 different websites.

2. Kalium

Perfectly suited to the blog or portfolio website, Kalium is one of the most popular. It is highly customizable with a free revolution slider, enabling you to create great looking slides. You can add custom transitions, effects, and animations, as well as choosing from several variations for portfolios. There are a lot of different styles to choose from and you get to control how much information is presented. You can link your personal website to it without having to create another account. More than 600 Google fonts are included and, all in all, it is a very easy theme to use, producing fantastic results.

3. Amax

This theme can be used for any website and is packed full of practical options. It has a modern design that will attract a lot of attention. Amax is a multipurpose theme and includes a number of very useful and flexible site-building tools. You can customize your fonts and colors and select multiple headers, layouts, and titles. You get creative control over your site, ensuring it will be unique.

There is a built-in composer that lets you design however many different pages you want on your site. If you don't want to design them all, there are built-in demos. There is also a video page building plugin included. Amax is highly responsive and optimized for all types of devices.

4. Divi

According to the creators of this theme, "the sky is the limit" and, should you choose to install Divi, you will see why. Divi offers unmatched functionality and customization features, of the kind that you will normally only get if you hire an expensive web designer. There is the Divi Builder, which helps you to create the perfect layout, allowing you to change anything and everything about the layout — colors, fonts, icons, page formats, and post formats, to name just a few. And, because it's a drag-and-drop builder, anyone can use it without needing to write any code.

There are also 18 layouts, which means you can install and upload to your website within an hour! The design is responsive and the whole theme is highly efficient. And, as an added feature, it will resize itself to fit any size screen, making it perfect for mobile devices regardless of operating system.

5. Azoom

Azoom is a very distinct and refreshing theme, designed for those who want consistency and good quality. It includes a long list of features, all designed to complement and enhance every web page. There are special grids that let you include parallax backgrounds, as well as other features designed to catch the eye of visitors.

Azoom also integrates Woo Commerce seamlessly, allowing you to add an online shop with your website, upping the functionality incredibly. There is a page builder, which lets you design great pages for your site, and, if you really do not want the work involved in starting from scratch, you can import demo content with the built in one click demo importer. You can also customize the page width without the need to access the code by using the theme options included.

6. Avada

This one works very well on any site, from a personal blog to a news site, a portfolio, or whatever your niche is. It is one of the best-selling themes, with more than 80,000 websites currently using it, but that does not mean they all look the same. The inclusion of Fusion Builder means that you can fully customize your site. This is a page builder that helps you to create a top unique layout in just a couple of hours.

There are also a number of premium sliders and five header designs included. Don't worry if you have no previous WordPress experience; Avada includes a full and dedicated support system, there whenever you need help or advice. This is the ideal choice for a website that is going to be selling services or products and is designed to work with Woo Commerce, Bottom Line and other ecommerce plugins.

7. Bridge

Bridge is another theme that can be used for any type of site, regardless of your niche or topic. It is packed full of features that are suitable for all sites and it is highly versatile. It is Retina-ready, so you can design your site around any device regardless of operating system.

The design and the code of Bridge are fully compatible with most e-commerce plugins, making it ideal for those who are setting up an online shop. The theme is simple, with drop-down menus, great icons, and built-in side menus, amongst many other features and design elements. It doesn't have a translator, but it is compatible with any of the WP multi-language packs, even those that are free.

The customization features let you create whatever layout you want and, using the drag-and-drop builder, you can pick and choose which elements you want to use and come up with a great layout in under 60 minutes. There are vectorial icons, more than 600 Google fonts, and a background slider so you can add multimedia content and four different animation effects. This is easily integrated for SEO purposes and is very SEO-friendly, resulting in more visitors to your website.

8. Salient

This one is all about the design. Salient offers you a very beautiful look for your website, helping you gain and retain traffic. What separates this theme from others is the inclusion of a video background, which is supported natively. When you first install the theme, you will notice that the color theme is dull, but this is designed to make you use the many customization options to make your site unique.

There are only two styles for blogs available and only one online shop style, but it is a nice-looking theme. There is a portfolio layout, which will enable you to display your work, and the customization options are quite impressive. You can change colors, layout, and typography to whatever you want. The design is highly responsive and is also Retina-ready. That means your site can be accessed and seen on any device. There are more than 350 Retina icons to choose from and eight different page layouts. You can choose between boxed or width for page style and this can be changed with just one button. When you change, all elements on the site change to adapt to the new style.

9. The7

This theme boasted more than 15,000 sales in just one year and, since it was first released, more than 100 bugs and features have been fixed or developed, respectively. The theme continues to improve every month and comes with plenty of free updates to keep you well and truly in the loop with the latest features. It is a multi-purpose theme and you can create a highly unique website using some of the customization options, like:

• Four header layouts

• Six skins that can easily be modified

• A number of home page layouts

• More than 600 Google fonts

• An unlimited color scheme

• Visual Composer plugin.

The Visual Composer plugin allows you to build whatever layout you want and is a great bonus, costing $14 if bought separately. You also get the premium versions of Go Responsive, Revolution Slider, and Compare Tables, as well as Layer Slider, all included free of charge.

It is a fully responsive theme and is simple and straightforward to use and customize.

10. Brooklyn

According to the creators of this theme, you will never need to buy another one. They say that Brooklyn offers all the customization options, and all the features a person could ever need in a multipurpose theme. It is modern looking, minimal, and elegant, as well as engaging. It was originally created for use as an interface on presentation sites, but a number of updates and development campaigns have made it into a premium theme. Instead of being just one, it is a number of themes all packaged together.

It is a highly responsive theme that works on any type of interface and operating system. You don't need to use any plugins to get a flawless and fast load speed, either. Included is a PS color action set that provides a great contrast between the background and your multimedia content.

It is used by beginners and experienced WordPressers alike, so if you have little to no experience, it isn't a problem with Brooklyn. Online video documentation is there to help you learn what to do from start to finish.

Between the free and the premium themes that I have detailed here, and the many thousands of others that are available on WordPress, there is nothing you can't do with your website. Give it any look you like, use any color scheme, any font, anything you like, and create a truly unique website.

Top 60 WordPress Plugins

Without WordPress plugins, your site would not work very well and would be, to be blunt, devoid of any functionality and, to a certain extent, of any personality as well. Plugins and widgets are available in the WordPress repository and there are hundreds to choose from — and if you want more you can buy premium ones as well.

It isn't just a case of picking any old plugin, though, because many of them will conflict with each other. If you notice an issue on your site after you have activated a new plugin, you need to deactivate it straightaway to see if it is the problem and delete it if needs be. And, if your chosen plugin does not work inside of an hour, get rid of it and choose another one.

The following are some of the best plugins available on WordPress, listed by functionality and most are free, although there are premium versions available if you want them.

ADVERTISING AND PROMOTION

1. AdRotate

Provides support for unlimited banner groups, which lets you tie in banners to specific parts of your site. You can also use the built-in geolocation to tie ads to parts of the world.

2. CTA Widget

A simple text widget that includes Image URL, Title, Link Text, a text/html area and Link URL.

3. Calls to Action

Allows calls to action to be created for your WordPress site and allows you to monitor conversion rates and improve them. Also lets you run A/B split tests and customize CTA templates, along with a lot more,

4. Go — Responsive Pricing and Compare Tables

This is for those who like to see a new generation of pricing table.

5. HMS Testimonials

Allows you to display testimonials on posts or pages. You can use grouping to display specific testimonials on the right page.

6. OptinMonster

A lead generation plugin that helps you create opt-in forms that grab the attention and convert.

COMMUNICATIONS

1. BuddyPress

This helps you to build up a social network for your business.

2. BP Group Hierarchy

Lets BuddyPress groups be added to other groups.

3. Recently Registered

On single-site WordPress, adds a sortable column to the users list so you can see the date of registration.

4. MailPoet Newsletters

Allows you to send newsletters, use auto-responders, and post notifications easily.

5. Subscribe2

When new posts are published on your blog, this plugin sends your subscribers a notification through email. With Readygraph integration, you can also automate user growth.

DESIGN

1. Column Shortcodes

Adds shortcodes to create columns on your pages or in posts.

2. Flexible Map

Allows you to embed Google Maps, either in your posts or on pages, using center coordinates, street address, or the URL to a KML file.

3. JetPack Custom CSS

Add or replace the CSS in your theme; includes syntax coloring, immediate feedback, and auto indentation.

4. JetPack Mobile

Mobile device users will automatically see the mobile version of your theme and can then choose to see the full site. Mobile theme can be enabled or disabled.

5. Widget Visibility

Controls visibility and is customized through a set of built in options.

6. Simple Page Sidebars

Assign custom sidebars to the pages of your choice without having to make any changes to the template.

7. Page Builder

Allows you to drag and drop your favorite widgets to build up a responsive layout for your pages.

8. Thrive Content Builder

A click-to-edit front-end builder.

9. WP Maintenance Mode

Gives you a splash page on your site that lets visitors know if your site is down for maintenance reasons.

10. Table Press

Allows you embed tables that are full of features in pages and posts without writing any code.

11. WPtouch Mobile Plugin

Enables a mobile theme automatically for mobile visitors to see when they visit your site.

ECOMMERCE

1. Woo Commerce

A powerful e-Commerce plugin that helps you sell just about anything.

2. Easy Digital Downloads

A complete plugin that lets you sell your digital downloads.

3. WordPress Simple PayPal Shopping Cart

An easy plugin to use that allows you to sell from your website with one click.

EVENTS

1. All-in-One Event Calendar

From Time.ly comes a plugin that gives you a complete calendar system, letting you see daily, weekly, and monthly views, along with agendas, upcoming events, and recurring events; and you can use color coding for certain categories. You can also import and export .ics feeds.

2. Booking Calendar

Manage bookings with an online system for reservations and availability checks.

3. Events Manager

Feature-rich event registration system includes locations management, recurrence, a calendar, booking management, and full integration of Google Maps.

4. WP Meetup

Allows events from Meetup.com to be shown on your blog, either in a calendar or through various widgets.

FORMS

1. Contact Form 7

Allows you to manage a number of contact forms and to customize the contents of the form and emails using simple markup.

2. Formidable Forms

Helps you to build forms using drag and drop and then lets you edit in place.

3. JetPack Contact Form

Customize your contact forms to suit your requirements and receive feedback when customers submit forms.

MAINTENANCE

1. Broken Link Checker

Checks your comments, posts, and all other content on your website for missing images and broken links, and tells you when any are found.

2. Duplicator

Helps you to make backups of your database and your WordPress files to duplicate your site and move it to another location in just a couple of simple steps. Also creates a snapshot, at any given point in time, of your website.

3. Simple Backup

Tools that help you optimize your website and back it up.

4. WP Backitup

Using a single click, you can create a ZIP file backup of your whole website. Backups are easy to archive and can also be easily downloaded for secure storage, away from your hosted site.

IMAGES

1. Advanced Image Styles

Adjust the border and margins of your images easily using the visual editor.

2. FlexSlider

Use shortcodes, widgets, or template tags to add responsive sliders and show blog posts, custom slides, or other content in responsive animated sliders.

3. JetPack Tiled Galleries

Show off your photos in a magazine style layout without the need for an external graphic editor.

4. NextGEN gallery

A very popular plugin for galleries, boasting more than 10 million downloads.

5. WP Smush It

Reduces image file sizes and improves the performance of your site.

SPEED

1. Hyper Cache

Formerly called Lite Cache, this plugin is designed to help you get the best speed for your website and can be used on both high-end servers and low-resource hosting.

2. WP Super Cache

This cache produces static HTML files from your dynamic blog. These are then served by the webserver instead of the much heavier and costlier WordPress PH scripts.

3. Query Strings Remover

Takes the query strings out of static CSS files, JavaScript files, and other static resources. Helps to improve cache performance and your overall Google PageSpeed score, as well as the scores on Pingdom, YSlow, and GTmetrix.

SECURITY

1. Akismet

This is an out-of-the-box plugin that comes with WordPress, and is the best way to keep your blog or website free of trackback or comment spam.

2. BulletProof Security

Helps protect your site from hundreds of thousands of different attempts and attacks from hackers.

3. Captcha

Adds a captcha plugin to your site for visitors to type in to prove they are not spam robots. The visitor will be asked to answer a math question.

4. Login Security Solution

Requires site visitors and users to have strong passwords, stops brute force attacks, stops login information disclosures, logs out idle sessions, lets admin know when there has been an attack and/or breach, and allows admin to disable logins for emergency or maintenance reasons and to reset everyone's passwords.

5. Sucuri Security

This provides activity auditing, security hardening, and SiteCheck, which scans for remote malware, spam, and other security issues. Also looks for post-hack issues and features.

SEARCH OPTIMIZATION

1. Google Analytics

Add Google analytics to your website, or blog easily with this plugin. Google analytics gives you loads of features, including search results, error page, and automatic outgoing links and it tracks downloads as well.

2. Google XML Sitemaps

Generates an XML sitemap that helps search engines index your website better.

3. JetPack Stats

Makes metrics easy to understand with a really nice interface.

4. WordPress SEO

An all-in-one solution for SEO, providing features such as sitemaps and content analysis, amongst many others.

SOCIAL

1. Floating Social Media Icon

Shows a floating social media icon, and allows you to configure the icon size, design, and order, as well as the support widget.

2. JetPack Publicize

Lets you easily share posts to social media sites, including Facebook, Tumblr, Twitter, LinkedIn, and Yahoo!

3. JetPack Sharing

Allows you to drag and drop social sharing services to the enabled section so they show up on your site.

4. Share Buttons

Puts share buttons on every page of your site so posts can be shared to Facebook, Google+, Twitter, Pinterest, and many more.

MISCELLANEOUS

1. Business Directory

Helps you build local directories, listings of business providers, review sections similar to Yelp, and yellow-page directories, as well as much more.

2. WP Directory Ninja

Helps you set up a niche or local directory website and pull targeted leads in.

3. S2Member Framework

A very powerful plugin for memberships that protects members' only content.

Chapter 5
Creating Posts

Creating your posts is important, because this is what really keeps visitors coming back for more. They want to make sure that you really know what you're talking about and that you are really going to be a benefit to them. If your posts don't convey enough information, it will cause problems for you, because your readers are going to decide that they really don't want anything to do with you or your website. They are going to turn to someone else who can give them the information they want.

So you need to make sure that your information is accurate and useful. If it's not, they won't keep reading. This might mean you need to do a little more research, even on topics that you thought you knew really well. You also need to keep your information interesting. No matter how smart you are, your readers are not going to keep reading your articles if they are just boring and full of information. They want to feel entertained and interested in the information as well. So include stories and firsthand accounts as well as some of the facts.

Visual and HTML

You will see two options, "Visual" and "HTML," at the right corner, just below the title. By default, WordPress will select "Visual." This option makes your entire workspace similar to Microsoft's Word, and it should be easy for you to create your posts. Granted that posting, editing, and formatting are easier in the Visual mode, you do not tap into the full potential of the formatting options that WordPress offers. This is available only in HTML, and knowing a little about HTML coding will help you go a long way (although it's not absolutely necessary, you can learn the basics fairly quickly). An example where HTML comes in handy will be mentioned in a while. With HTML, you can create custom fields and custom block quotes, which make your blog or website look richer and unique, and display your efforts to maintain your blog.

Now you really need to know how to create a post through WordPress. It's actually not as difficult as you might think.

Just go to the page that says "new post." You will see a screen in the center that looks very familiar if you've ever used Microsoft Word. You need to create a title for the top of the page before you begin. Make sure that the title will get someone's attention and that it's easy to read. You don't want something too long, (unless you're writing a scientific blog) because it's more difficult for your readers to understand, and they won't want to read through the article if they can't even understand the title.

Right under the title is your web address. This will be the specific address for this particular article, so it's important that you pay attention to it. Make sure that you make the address short, to the point, and easy to understand. This means that it should be no more than three to five words long. You can change the default address (which is the entire title of the article) by clicking the button to edit right next to this address. Then shorten your topic to a few words. This ensures that the reader knows what the article is about, but that they aren't too thrown off by the long address, and can't find the article again later.

Once you've created these two pieces, you should create the actual content. Make sure that you keep the content interesting and that you keep it in blocks of text. This is going to make it easier for the reader when they read your information. Breaking things up with headings or bullet points (or even pictures) is also going to help. These things make the content much easier for someone to read, which means they are much more likely to continue reading it after they start. You can format all the information in the same way that you would format a Microsoft Word page, as all the same information is found at the top of the screen. This makes it simple to take care of this aspect of content creation.

Add Media

You can easily add images or gifs with the "Add Media" button at the top left. This opens a window showing images that you uploaded to your library. You can also add new images from your computer, or just click on "Add via URL" and give the URL of the image. This uploads the image to the location of your cursor. You can resize the image to whichever orientation you want and you have the option of aligning it to the left, center or right. As soon as the image is uploaded into the workspace, you will be able to see a little text box below the image in grey color. This box is where you will be typing out your caption, and the caption can be formatted the same way as the normal text can.

Add/Edit Link

You can also link to another website and give a different link text. Just click on the "Add/Edit Link" button and fill out the text boxes, and you are good to go. This is particularly useful when you want to link to a lengthy URL. You can just link the URL with a word in your blog. When audience visitor clicks the name, they will be directed to the website you linked. It also makes your blog look professional, and it is recommended to spend the extra few seconds.

Block Quote and Insert Read More

Next up are block quotes and the "Insert Read More" tag. Block quotes are generally used when you want to quote more than three to four lines. It can make your blog look fancy, but WordPress comes only with the default straight-line block quote in visual mode. You need to do a little bit of HTML coding to customize your block quotes. We'll discuss that in more detail later. When the "Insert Read More" tag is used, you show the viewer only the beginning of the post, and he has to click the "Continue Reading" option to read more. You can edit it to say something other than "Continue Reading" as well. Simply switch to HTML mode, and replace the "Continue Reading" in the "<!- - more Continue Reading - ->" part with a phrase of your choice. This is a teaser of sorts to the reader.

These are the formatting options that are different from those in Word. The remaining options are quite easy to use and you should have no trouble with them.

Excerpts

Excerpts are most commonly confused with teasers. The excerpt of a post is just a condensed form of the blog post. When users search in Google, it displays your excerpt, and when you search someone's categories, it displays the excerpt along with the title. Therefore, your excerpt should be precise, interesting and at the same time, should not give away the entire content of your blog. It is what decides if you get the reader's attention or not.

Click on *More Options* and the "Excerpt" text box will be displayed.

Pingbacks and Trackbacks

You will be able to see this option (which is checked by default) under *More Options*. When a blogger posts his own blog, but links to your blog somewhere in his post, then you get pingback in your comment sections, which you can approve.

A trackback is slightly different. If a blogger sees your blog and wants to share his opinion, all he/she needs to do is post a comment. IF the blogger wants his own audience to see his comment, he/she can create a related blog post separately, and send a trackback to your blog. You will receive the trackback request in your comment, which will be a permalink, and you can accept it so your viewers can read the other blogger's post as well. However, you have the authority to edit the excerpt of the other blogger's post that appears in your comment section.

Next, as you scroll down further you will find a section for a meta description as well as sections for your keywords. This is where you're going to need a little bit more information. A meta description is a very short (155-character maximum) description of what can be found on your page. You want it to give a little blurb that will draw readers in, but you have to do it carefully because you only have a small amount of space. This is the little blurb that shows up under the webpage title when you search for something on Google. Make it count.

Your keywords are words that describe your article. If you wrote about the best dog collar then you might use keywords like "dog, collar, top collar, best collar," etc. These are words that people would search for when looking for information that you are posting. Now, this is very similar to the tags feature, which allows you to tag your article for a reader to search it more easily. The keywords are used on your website so, when someone searches your website, they will find this particular article. Tags are for the web in general. That means when someone searches Google they will find it.

You can also ad other components to your web page, such as a featured image that shows up next to the article title when it's posted to the web page. If you want, you can select a specific time for your post to go live as well. This is great if you are going to be gone for a period of time or if you don't want to have to come back to your website every day. Instead of posting a new article each day or week, you can create a store of articles, and schedule them to post at the same time every week.

To do this, click on the small calendar icon next to "Publish." A calendar pops up, where you can select the date and time. Your post will go live at the specified time.

Note that WordPress uses standard GMT timings, so fill in the details accordingly (WordPress does tell you the time difference between your zone and GMT, so this should not be too much of a problem).

Make sure that you preview your posts as well. Right up at the top in the corner is going to be a button that says *Preview Post*. You can look at your page as a reader would see it by going to that page. This will help you see if there are any problems with your formatting, with text, pictures, or anything else. And you can make sure that everything is perfect before you go to the trouble of posting and getting complaints or realizing there's a problem and being forced to take the page down to fix it.

Top Tips for Turning Out the Perfect Blog Post

Anyone can write, but not everyone can write well. One of the keys to success on your blog or website is turning out good quality content that makes sense and that keeps people reading, wanting to know more. The following tips will help you to write the perfect blog post, and the same tips can be used for normal website content as well.

Understand Your Audience

Before you sit down to write your blog post, make sure you understand your target audience. Ask yourself what they want to read about and what information they want. Think about what you know about your buyers and their interests before you put pen to paper.

For example, if your blog is aimed at millennials who want to start an online business, you really don't need to talk about social media because most of them probably know more about it than you do! What you could do, though, is talk about changing their approach to social media from a personal friendly tone to one that is more tailored to business. That is what will set you apart from the ones that just churn out generic information — telling your audience what they want and need to hear, not what they already know.

Start with a Topic and Working Title

Before you can go anywhere with your blog post, you need to have a good topic and a working title ready. You can start with a general topic and then, later on, focus on a particular aspect, which will help you to write your title. A working title is very specific and will be the guide that takes you through the post.

Start with your topic; from that, you can write your working title, and if this is going to be the end, you will then come up with your final title — more about those later on.

Write a Captivating Introduction

Your first few sentences have to grab your readers' attention. If they don't, or if your readers get bored early on, they won't read any further, which means your post doesn't get much attention.

The best way to grab their attention is to start with a story or a joke, show a bit of empathy, or quote an interesting statistic or fact. Then go on to describe what you are hoping to achieve with the post, and how it is going to address a specific problem that a reader might be experiencing. This gives them a reason to continue reading and tells them how what you are writing about will improve things for them.

Organize Your Content

On occasion, there can be quite a lot of information in a blog post, for both the writer and the reader. You need to organize the information in a logical manner so that readers are not put off by the length of the post, or the amount of information in it. You can organize things in a number of different ways — a list, sections, tips, whatever works best.

Use bullet points to split the information up and use headings throughout the post so that it doesn't look like one big lump of never-ending text. If it still looks too much, split the sections into subsections. The trick is to make it look like several posts in one, breaking the content up into manageable chunks. To do this, draw up an outline of the post so you can see where the sections should be.

Get Writing

This is a pretty obvious step, but it is by no means the last one! Now that you have an outline of what you want to write, and you have your working title, it's time to write the actual content. Using your outline, expand on each point as necessary. Write about what you know and, where you need clarification, make sure you do plenty of research to get the information you need, including examples and statistics. Make sure that, if you use external sources, you attribute them to the author correctly — that goes for images, as well.

Edit and Proofread, Then Format

You are close to creating the perfect post, but there are a couple more steps. The first is to proofread your work. Make sure it flows well, makes sense, and doesn't contain any grammatical or spelling errors. Make edits where necessary, but don't remove any important information. Once you are happy with the content, check the formatting, looking at the following:

Your Featured Image

Choose an image that looks appealing and is relevant to your content. Social networks tend to target content that has images, giving them more preferences and displaying them more prominently. Because of that, images are vital to the success of your blog when it comes to social media. Data also shows that emails sent with images are preferred over those that don't have them, so including an image in newsletters or emails sent to your subscribers is also important.

The Visual Appearance

No one likes to look at ugly posts, and pictures aren't the total answer, either. If your post is not formatted properly and is all over the place, it won't look good. That's where using headers and sub-headers come into its own, especially when they are all consistent. Take a step back and look at the layout of your blog objectively — if necessary, get someone else to do it. Then make the changes needed to tidy up.

Topics and Tags

Tags are public-facing keywords, specifically those that are used to describe a particular post. They let your readers look for relevant content in the category you have written about. Do not add a whole list of tags to each post; use a good strategy and choose between 10 and 20 that are representative and relevant to the main topics that your blog covers.

Make Sure Your Blog Ends with a Call to Action — CTA

Every blog post should end with a CTA. This indicates what your readers should do next — it could be subscribing to your blog, purchasing or downloading an eBook, reading something else that is related, signing up for a webinar — you get the idea. Think of the CTA as being beneficial to you. Once your readers have read the post, they should want to click on the CTA, and that potentially generates a lead for you. You should also use the CTA to add more content that is beneficial for your readers.

Optimize for On-Page SEO

Once you have completed the writing and formatting, it's time to optimize things for the search engines. Don't get hung up on how many keywords need to be in there. Simply make sure that you use the RIGHT keywords, the ones that you are targeting, and do make sure that they are used in a way that doesn't have a negative impact on the reader. Your post must not read like spam, and it must not be packed with keywords just for the sake of it — Google and the other major search engines are a little more intelligent than that! Here are some tips on how to do this properly:

Meta Description

These are the descriptions you see on Google, underneath the result title. They help people who are searching to see a summary of the content before they click to read a post, and are usually between 150 and 160 characters long. They should start with a verb, such as "Discover," "Read," or "Learn." Meta descriptions are not taken into account by Google anymore when they are looking at keyword ranking, but they are important for your readers to see what they will get out of reading your post. They can also help your search click-through rate.

Page Title and Headers

A lot of the blogging software out there will use the title of your post as your page title, and this is very important when it comes to on-page SEO. However, if you have carefully followed everything I've written so far, you already have a title that includes keywords and/or key phrases that your audience wants and is interested in. Don't get too complicated with that title; don't fit keywords in where they really don't belong. That said, if there is a clear opportunity to add relevant and targeted keywords to the title and headers of your post, then go ahead and do it. Do try to keep headlines and sub-headers short and to the point, otherwise they will get truncated in the search results.

Anchor Text

These are the words or phrases that will link to another page on your website or another site. Be careful about which words you choose to link to that site, because anchor text is taken into account by search engines for keyword ranking. You should also consider which page you are linking to. Think about linking to pages that you want well ranked for a particular keyword — do this right and you might just end up on Page 1 of the Google search results.

Mobile Optimization

People tend to use their mobile devices more than desktops these days, which makes it vital that your site is optimized for the mobile device. More than 70% of those asked in recent research said that they would return to a site if it had been optimized for mobile, and because of this Google takes mobile optimization seriously when they are ranking you, and they also tend to prioritize sites that are fully responsive, or optimized.

Pick a Catchy Title

Finally, it's time to finish off that working title you produced at the beginning. The following formula will help you to come up with a title that is catchy and attention grabbing:

• Begin with your working title.

• Edit the title and, as you do, bear in mind that your final title must be clear and accurate.

• Make your title sexy by using strong language or alliteration or some other way.

• Try and get some keywords in to the title, but make sure they fit naturally.

• Shorten it if you can. Nobody likes to see a long title and Google tends to prefer those that are 65 characters or less.

Follow these tips to produce a winning blog, one that people want to read and that keeps their attention. The idea of the blog post is also to make people want to come back and read your next one, or any other content that you may post on your site, so keep that in mind when you are writing, as well.

Chapter 6
Customizing Your Website

You now have a good idea of what your website should look like. You can now create your posts, give them some formatting, and create taglines and other elements. It is time to take things one step further; yes, you should now customize your website or blog to make it truly your own. You ought to change your default background, create pages, add widgets, and, most important, change your theme. Themes are the first thing you should change, as they decide the overall format of your website. With a pleasant theme, your readers would be hooked. A few themes have already been discussed, and you should select from these top trending themes when you start out. Most of the options needed to customize your website can be found under the "Appearance" and "Settings" tabs in your *Dashboard* when you log in as the admin.

Depending on the theme you select, your sidebar will be placed either to the left or the right. It would be better to select a theme that places your sidebar on the right, as it makes things easier for the reader. Having the content on the right and sidebar on the left creates discomfort to reader.

With all that said, let's move on to the different things you can customize in the "Appearance" tab:

Background

From your admin page, go to *Appearance -> Background*. This should bring up the background customization page. Different themes offer different ways to customize your background, so you might want to play around first (preferably in your localhost) to see which background fits your content best. If the available images aren't quite what you expected, you can create your own custom background. Simply click on "Add Image" and upload the image you want into your Media Library, then select it. This changes your background, giving it a custom feel.

Header

Headers are images that appear right next to your blog name (or your blog name may appear over the header, in some themes). By default, your header will not have any image selected. Go to *Appearance -> Header* and add a new image. The recommended pixel size varies from theme to theme (and should be followed), but it is not necessary to stick to those numbers. Once you upload the image and crop it, hit "Save" and voila! Your website now has a beautiful header to support your content.

Pages

Creating a page is different from creating a post, as you want the content in a page to remain static. A good example of a page would be "About Me," where you give a few details about yourself. This content never changes, hence you want it to be a page and not a post. If you need certain posts to appear in the sidebar no matter where the reader is in your website, creating them as a page instead of a post would be a good idea. Ideally, having a blog, forums, and a news page would mean your followers have easy access to the most visited parts of your website.

Creating a page is very easy - go to your admin page and click on "Add New." A page similar to the one where you create posts will appear and you can customize the page the same way you would a post.

However, a few things are different when compared to posts. On the right side, you can see "Page Attributes." This allows you to group a few pages together, under one page, and order it alphabetically (default). You can create your own order by using corresponding numbers in the "Order" toolbox. Select the page you want as the parent page from the "Parent" dropdown list.

Great! Now you have created your own page and published it. But there is a small catch. The page doesn't appear on your website! No, it is not a glitch; you just need to add the page widget. The next section covers another important part of your website - Widgets.

Widgets

Widgets are just tools to make reading your website pleasurable and easier. Go to *Appearance -> Widgets* to open the Widgets page. Here you can see a list of available widgets on the left side, and a *Sidebar* on the right. If you want a particular widget, drag it from the left and drop it on the *Sidebar*. The widget now appears in your website.

Some important widgets are "About Me," "Pages," "Categories," "Follow Blog," "Search," and "Facebook." These widgets will allow you to organize your website and they make it possible for you to share it in your social media platform. You can also choose which widget you want in a particular page or post. You can customize this, by clicking on *Appearance -> Widgets*, then "Screen Options" at the top right corner. Now click on the link that appears and you can start customizing the appearance of your widgets on individual pages.

Menu

Menus offer a great way to organize your pages. A menu is basically a page with several subpages. These subpages can have their own subpages and so on. Usually, you get two menus, primary and social. You should make use of the primary menu to link the different parts of your blog that you want your follower to see, and the social menu to link to your social media platforms. Most themes place your menu in the sidebar

Click on *Appearance -> Menu* to enter the Menu page. Create your first menu after giving it a name. You won't get the name of the menu on the website; instead you'll have the name of the first page you've added. You can add pages to your menu by selecting them on the left side, and clicking on "Add to Menu." You can also add posts the same way. Now, if you take a look at your website, all the pages you selected will be grouped together and displayed, instead of the usual dropdown style that you would have expected. To fix this, you need to create subpages. Go to the Menu page, and click and hold on the page you want to be a subpage. Simply drag it a bit to the right and release. This page is now a subpage to the previous page. You can create multiple subpages for a single page. Drag the page a bit more to the right for it to become a subpage to a subpage.

As previously mentioned, using Social menu to link your Facebook, Twitter, and/or Google+ accounts would be a good way to let your readers know you're available in social media platforms as well. To do this, create a new menu, uncheck "Primary Menu" at the bottom, and leave "Social Menu" checked. Now go to "Custom Links" on the left side, and paste the URL of your social media platform here, then give a "Link Text" to make it look better and hide the actual link address. Add it to the menu, save, and you're all set! You can link any number of websites you want, and it's not limited to just social media. You can link websites even in your Primary Menu.

You can create several menus, but your theme would most likely support only two (if it's a free theme). In this case, you have the choice of selecting the menu you want as the Primary Menu and Social Menu. Some themes do, however, offer you more than two menus and you can use them all to help organize your website better. It depends on the theme, but sometimes you can change the location of your menu to the top instead of the side, which makes your website look even better.

These are some of the customizations you can make from the *Appearance* tab. Let's now move into the *Settings* tab:

Blog Icon

You can create a blog icon, which is a small picture that appears next to your blog post in the WordPress website. This is a great way to let people know who you are and recognize you and your posts. Go to *Settings -> General*, and you will be able to see the "Blog Picture/Icon" on the right. Upload your image, then crop it and hit "Save."

While you're here in the general settings, you can also edit your website's title, tagline, time zone, and date and time formats. They aren't absolutely necessary, but these small accurate changes here and there help display you as a dedicated blogger.

Reading and *Discussions*

The *Reading* tab settings affect the readability of your website. You can decide which post or page appears on your front page (extremely important, as it decides whether the viewer reads or grieves), how many posts a blog page can show, visibility of your website, and much more. If you are looking to make some money off your website, it's important to check the "Allow Search Engines to index this site." By doing this, you are permitting a search engine to display your website in the search page. With the proper titles and tagline (and proper content, of course), your website or blog may be the first result on the search engine. You are guaranteed to make some passive money if your website ends up in the top five search results.

The *Discussion* tab gives you settings that allow you to control everything follower-related. You can decide if you want notifications whenever you get a comment or a link to another website, or if the follower needs to get your approval for posting a comment. Allowing a follower who has a previously approved comment is a better choice than manually approving each comment, as it is tiring and a pointless waste of time.

Sharing

How you want your followers to share your website is completely up to you. With the *Sharing* tab, you can select which social media platforms you want your followers to follow you on, and you can even customize the appearance of these sharing icons. You can have either the platform's icon alone, or the name alone, or both together. You can play around with the settings to figure out what's best for your website. You can go for appearance but, more important, you should be aiming to make it easier for your followers to share your posts and follow you on social media. This ensures that they keep coming back for more.

Apart from these options, there are options like "Polls," which allows you host a poll in which you ask a question and allow the follower to choose an answer, and "Ratings," which allows followers to rate your pages and posts. You can choose whether you want the rating results to be displayed above or below a blog post. Placing your ratings above would be beneficial only if you have a high rating.

When it comes to customizing your website, you should think from a reader's point of view. Using lots of images and fancy fonts in your posts may give your website a unique appearance, but there are certain ubiquitous customizations that help direct traffic to your website. You get more traffic only if you get the reader to stay after his visit to your website. Have the reader's thoughts and expectations in mind when you design your website. Placing the text on the left with the sidebar on the right ensures that your reader will not be distracted and can read the blog post easily. If you want to create a website with a language in which you write from right to left, then you want to do the opposite with the sidebar.

With these tips in mind and instructions at hand, you can develop a blog that not only attracts readers, but also gets them interested enough to keep coming back. If you have a subscription plugin, you will definitely get more hits if you are consistent and creative with your website. These are not the only ways to create a solid, well-received blog. Read on to know more about developing your blog and giving it a professional touch.

Chapter 7

Developing Your Blog

Now that you've figured out how to make posts and pages on WordPress, you're ready and able to get started with the blog itself. There are a few things to keep in mind when you start your blog, and it all starts with your topic. Remember, you were supposed to develop your topic at the beginning of this book, before you started creating your theme and your design. That's going to be important as you start creating your specific content.

In order to truly develop your blog, you need to understand some of the key things that are required for any type of website to get some readers, and make sure that they find the content they are looking for. You need to make sure that you are using different skills in SEO as well as organization. These things are going to make it possible for your readers and potential new readers to reach out to you, and to find more information about the topics and interests that they have.

SEO means "search engine optimization." When you go to Google, Yahoo, Bing, or any other search engine, and you type a word or phrase in to the search, you're contributing to this process. That word you used is a keyword or a key phrase. Other people do this too, otherwise search engines simply wouldn't work. The search engine compiles the words that you used and searches for websites that use those words multiple times, also taking into account how good the content is, the types of reviews that site has, and how many similar words it uses. The website with the highest ranking overall will show up at the top of the search results page.

Now some keywords and phrases are searched more than others. What you want to do is find out what the best ones are for your particular topic area. Several websites will provide you with the ability to search phrases and keywords. What you want to do is find keywords that are searched frequently, but not necessarily the top words in your area. These top words are going to have a lot of websites fighting over them, and it can be difficult to get in. Instead, go for some of the mid-range words. You'll be able to see the rankings of how often those words are searched by creating your own list and running it through the search engines.

Once you run through your potential keywords, you'll be able to see the ones that you want to use pretty easily. Make sure you have a few keywords to focus on (these are the ones you want to try and use in each article) and a few more that you can intersperse when appropriate or when necessary. These words are going to be used throughout a number of your articles, and you want to make sure that you're picking the right ones. You need to keep several other things in mind at the same time however.

One important thing is that search engines are now capable of scanning your content for readability and usefulness. What that means is that they are able to tell if your content is actually going to help someone, or if it's just keyword stuffing. In the past, many people would create websites that didn't have a lot of information on them, but contained articles that were really just keywords over and over. This was generally a ploy to get readers to purchase a product, or to click through to a different website.

The problem with this was readers started to get annoyed and upset, so the search engines had to make a few changes. They had to create a way to understand what the actual information was in the articles and how useful it was. So now you are not able to use keyword stuffing. You need to use your keywords a good number of times so the search engine picks it up, but you need to avoid using them too much or giving up some of the quality for more appearances of that keyword. 1%-5% max is usually all you want for keywords.

Make sure that your content is high quality as well. This is extremely important because it improves your ranking on search engines, and it will increase your readership in a few different ways. First, you'll show up higher on search engine results, so more people will find you. Second, you're going to have more of your readers come back to your site because they know what they're getting. Third, you'll have a lot more readers (and maybe even other websites in your field) recommending you and drawing in more readers.

As you start gaining more followers, creating and editing content alone can become quite demanding. If you would like to hire a few people to do particular tasks with you watching over them, it's completely possible with

WordPress! You can assign different roles to the people you've hired. These roles come predefined within WordPress and their functions are also fixed. Make sure to invite and hire only those whom you trust or know personally, as some roles give enough authority to delete your posts.

The available roles are:

- Administrator

- Editor

- Author

- Contributor

- Viewer

- Follower

Administrator

To the administrator, everything is within limits. He can control everything in the website, including content, background, themes, etc. He also has the power to change a person's role.

Editor

The editor can do everything when it comes to posts and pages, including deleting them. Therefore, it is important that you have someone you trust as an editor, because it is not considered as a hack if the editor decides to sabotage your website by deleting all your posts.

Author

The author has similar authority as that of an editor, but only on *his* posts. He cannot edit posts that are not his own. As such, if you were hiring people to create content, giving them the position of Author would be best.

Viewer

The viewer simply reads your posts and leaves comments. He can do nothing other than this (besides mailing you, if you have the mailing widget enabled).

Follower

A follower is different from a viewer. When you have a private blog or website, then the readers you have are followers, as you have to personally invite them for them to be able to see your posts and pages. They have the same privileges as a viewer.

To invite a person and assign him a role, go to *Users ->*
Invite New on the Dashboard and enter the details. Choose
the role you want to assign, and type out a message
requesting the person to become the role. Then, click on
"Send Invitation" to invite him. To edit the roles of your
members, go to *Users -> All Users* and make the
appropriate changes with the help of the checkboxes and
dropdown lists next to the person's name.

Chapter 8
Keeping Readers

The first page to create is one that's all about you. This one will introduce you as an expert in your field, and it will help everyone around you understand why they should be coming to you and your blog to get more information and to get the advice that they need to be successful. You need to make sure you share some of your history, your education or work experience, your personal experiences, or anything else that's going to help people in your specific area believe that you're the best.

As you continue to develop new information, and continue to advance in your blog you'll be able to create articles that are based more on your topic instead of yourself. The first few articles, though, are going to be important in establishing yourself. Consider this: If you were going to listen to someone about this topic what would you want to know about them? That's what you need to explain in the first few weeks while also starting out with a few news stories or forum questions that will get your readers more involved with your blog right from the start.

Your next few articles should focus on specific areas of interest. Try to focus on some of the most interesting topics in your field. This is going to draw in a lot more people, because they're likely to be searching these things more frequently. You want to make sure that the blog is appealing to readers so make sure that you continue to check your forum for more information on what your readers really want to know about. If you run out of ideas this is a great way to come up with some new article titles as well.

Keeping readers is going to require you to have consistent content. That means you need to stay on top of the news in the field or area that you're writing about. You need to make sure that, whatever else is going on, you get that information onto your website as quickly as possible. That's how you're going to keep the readers interested and coming back to you, because they will know that you are the first person to go to when they want to know about the current situation of that topic.

Even if your topic doesn't make the actual news often (maybe you like to write about quilting or raising honeybees), that doesn't mean there isn't some type of news in that field. Has a new product come out recently that makes gathering honey easier? Maybe there's a new pattern that's becoming quite popular. These things are going to be news to someone that's interested in your topic. They are also going to interest your readers and keep them coming back to learn more about whether you've tried out the new product, or technique and what you have to say about it.

If you want to make some money with your blog, it's actually quite easy to do. You'll need to spend a little money first, because you need your own host, but then you can use your website however you want. You will be able to put ads on the site and gain revenue that way, choose click-through ads with revenue generation, and even create partnerships with companies that create products in your field to help you gain a little profit every time someone from your site clicks through and purchases a product from them. It's a great way to make a little extra on the side.

On the other hand, if you want to make a little more money, you can also consider creating your own products, and selling them on your website. Make sure that if you do decide to promote products, or if you decide to make your own you look into them first. You need those products to be high quality, or you could lose credibility with your current readers. That's going to lose money instead of helping you make it. By checking out everything first, you can save yourself the struggle.

Keep in mind, no matter what you do, that it's much easier to build up your empire and your followers the first time around. If you lose those readers, it's going to be nearly impossible to gain them back. Once you lose their trust and they feel like you're not a good person for that field anymore, it's hard to bring them back to you. After all, you're supposed to be the expert. They are likely to believe the things you tell them because of that fact and it can result in problems in the long run.

Make sure you're developing your blog well and that you're creating useful content and building a reader base before you worry about earning a lot of money. Most companies will require that you have some type of reader base before they'll even consider selling products through you, so you need to work your hardest on creating a user-friendly website (WordPress will help with that), creating useful content and just being reliable and trustworthy. Once you manage this, you're going to be well on your way to a larger readership, and possibly even a little extra money on the side just for doing something that you love to do.

12 Top Tips for Driving Relevant Traffic to Your Website

Traffic is the single most important factor that will keep your blog alive and give you a reason for all the hard work you have put in. Unfortunately, building the blog is the easy bit. What if you are getting lots of traffic to your blog but you are not particularly happy with the type of traffic it is? Maybe your visitors disappear as soon as they open your page. These are not the kind of visitors you want. What you are after is targeted traffic, and that is not easy to get. The idea behind this section is to give you some tips that will help you to drive relevant traffic to your website.

1. Use Social Media

Using social media is one of the smartest things you can do to drive targeted traffic to your website. Not only is it another place where you can publish your posts, it's a way of keeping followers of your site completely up to date about what's going on. And you don't have to stick to just sharing your posts, either. Share anything that is relevant and start up conversations just to get people talking. This also lets them get to know the real you.

There are a lot of auto-sharing tools you can use to make things a bit easier for you, including a plugin we mentioned earlier called JetPack Publicize. Tools like this save you a lot of time and they also allow you to put automatic scheduling on your updates. However, you should always add a custom message — never post a link without something that makes it more personal.

In addition, make sure that you give your readers a way of sharing your content by installing social sharing buttons at the end of each post by using the relevant WordPress plugin. The following are the most popular:

ShareThis — Great for those who want a simple button. Choose from more than 120 social channels, including Twitter, Facebook, Pinterest, etc.

Shareaholic — This is great for people who run a really trendy site. You can also add the related posts feature at the end of your posts, allowing you to link to other content related to the post.

Flare — If you want a share bar that is floating and horizontal, this one is for you. It also allows you to put your share buttons at the top or the bottom of your content.

Pin it! Button - Ideal for those who put a lot of creative pictures and content on their websites, it allows people to pin it to their Pinterest account.

2. Add a Newsletter Signup Form

Adding a mailing list or newsletter sign-up form is a brilliant way to get repeat visitors. Email newsletters let you expand your relationship with those who subscribe to you by sending them regular updates and adding the personal touch.

Do make sure that your newsletters are relevant, useful, and interesting to your subscribers. If you continually send emails full of adverts and content that has no bearing on your website, your subscribers will soon remove their names from your list — and, more important, they won't recommend your site to anyone else. You can get software to help you with email marketing to make life easier for you. Do make sure that your newsletters are sent out on a regular basis, otherwise you will lose the interest of your visitors and subscribers.

1. Post Quality Content on a Regular Basis

Everyone loves to see fresh content. Let's face it, you don't like reading the same old stuff over and over again, and neither do your visitors. For that matter, the search engines don't much like it either. Make sure visitors have a reason to come back to your site by updating on a regular basis with fresh new content. Make sure it is unique, relevant, and interesting. You can add visual aids, like videos and photographs, as long as they are related to your content. And you should also make use of whitespace. Generally, people don't actually read content, they scan it. They are looking for the information that is relevant to them, so use short paragraphs or lists, or split your post into sections with relevant and interesting headings.

3. Optimize Your Content for Search Engines

This has to be one of the best ways to boost traffic streams to your website or blog. Optimizing your site for SEO means that search engines are more likely to pick it up and rank it. Each separate piece of content on your website or blog must be optimized separately; here's how to do it:

Use the Meta Title and Description Properly. These should be short, relevant, and unique. Add at least a couple of targeted and valuable keywords. Keep the length of your title to about 60 characters and the meta description to about 150 to 160 characters. Look for good WordPress plugins (I mentioned a couple above) to help you customize your title and description for each piece of content on the blog.

Google Authorship. To improve your search result visibility, use Google Authorship. Having a good and professional looking image beside each post will improve not only your search engine ranking credibility, but it will also reward you with a much higher click-through rate than you would get without it — and that's what it's all about.

Related Posts. At the end of each post, add a list of related posts to keep your visitors on your site for longer. If your website has been set up well, the longer they stay, the more chance there is of them signing up to your newsletter or subscribing to your blog. Again, look for WordPress plugins that will help you do this easily.

Link Internally. Add links to other pages on your site within each post, but make sure they are relevant links. This gets link juice spread much further across your domain and it increases your visibility and the potential for more traffic.

4. Link Building for SEO

Use the Right Categories and Tags. This is important — WordPress allows you to select tags and categories for each separate post. Don't overdo it or you will look like nothing more than a spammer, and the search engines hate spammers with a passion. Stick to between three and five tags.

Image ALT Tags. Add one of these to every image that you upload to your website. These are used to describe the image and are very useful for ranking in the search engines. Again, keep the descriptions relevant and, if it fits naturally, get a keyword in there as well.

Anchor Text. Make sure your anchor text includes targeted keywords.

Nice Permalinks. Try to modify the settings for your permalinks to those that are SEO friendly. For example, a bad permalink for a post entitled "How to Blog" would have the website name followed by "/?p=25." A good one would have "/how-to-blog at the end." You can change these through "Settings" and "Permalinks," then clicking on "Post Name."

Structure of the Headings Tags. These must be structured properly if they are to work for SEO. Most of you have heard of H1, H2, H3, etc. — these are the headings tags and they should be used in numerical order. Apply these rules when you are formatting your post:

• H1 always goes before H2, H2 before H3, and so on.

• H1 is the main title. H2 and II3, etc., are for sub-headings.

• Only use H1 once. The rest can be used as often as necessary, but don't abuse that rule.

• Do include targeted keywords in your tags.

• You don't need to use all 6 H tags — so long as you have H1 and H2, which will be enough.

The main search engine is Google, which has more than 3 billion people using it every single day. If you want your site to be found by Google, make sure your content is worth reading and everything is formatted correctly.

5. Use Breadcrumbs

For those that don't know, breadcrumbs are a kind of trail, made from links that are generally placed at the top of the pages. They show the current location and let you track pages you looked at previously. Google takes breadcrumbs very seriously when it comes to ranking, so make sure you use them properly. Your visitors will also know where on your website they are. If a breadcrumb topic interests them, they will click on it and that helps to reduce bounce rate.

6. Use Keywords Effectively

Keywords, keywords, keywords. The backbone of SEO, but only when used properly. If you use the right keywords with the right density and in the right place, your blog posts will rank much higher in the search listings. Put yourself in the place of a searcher — think about what you would search for and make sure your keywords, or key phrases, are inserted throughout your posts correctly. Here's how to do that:

In Your Post Title

You must be very specific when you are coming up with your post titles. Let's say your post is about a film that aired in 2004, called **Crash.** Instead of just calling your post "Crash," you should use a title like "Crash 2004 — Movie

Review" or something similar. The word "Crash" on its own is way too broad and will get you nowhere fast.

In Your Post

Adding relevant keywords does tell the search engines what your content is about, but do shy away from keyword stuffing. Your keywords must fit naturally with the content. Search engines do not like keyword stuffing and, if you don't know what it is, the following definition comes direct from Google:

"Keyword stuffing" refers to the practice of loading a webpage with keywords or numbers in an attempt to manipulate a site's ranking in Google search results. Often these keywords appear in a list or group, or out of context (not as natural prose). Filling pages with keywords or numbers results in a negative user experience, and can harm your site's ranking. Focus on creating useful, information-rich content that uses keywords appropriately and in context.

Examples of keyword stuffing include:

Lists of phone numbers without substantial added value

Blocks of text listing cities and states a webpage is trying to rank for

Repeating the same words or phrases so often that it sounds unnatural, for example:

"We sell custom cigar humidors. Our custom cigar humidors are handmade. If you're thinking of buying a custom cigar humidor, please contact our custom cigar humidor specialists at <u>custom.cigar.humidors@example.com</u>."

There are tools available to help you with your keywords, so make good use of them to make sure that Google doesn't down rank your site.

7. Start Making Friends Online

Use the most powerful tool there is — social media — to spread the word. Get involved in conversations with people who have the same hobbies and interests as you do. Use all of the social media sites you can, including Facebook, Twitter, Pinterest, LinkedIn, and Google+. Don't overlook online forums in your niche either, as these can be valuable resources, but don't just use them for information. Actively contribute and you will get far more value out of it.

Visit the blogs and websites of people you make friends with in these places and leave comments on their posts — meaningful ones!

8. Be a Guest Blogger

Guest blogging is a great way to maximize your visibility and encourage more people to visit your web site. Guest blog only in places that are relevant to your niche, and make sure that you are writing for a website that produces and provides good quality content. You won't always be allowed to guest blog on a site, but don't be put off by rejections. Be persistent without being a nuisance. Someone will say yes, sooner or later.

9. Get Involved in Q&A Sites

There are a few of them out there, like Quora, Answers.com, and Yahoo! Answers. Answer only questions that are of high quality and those that you can truly answer with valuable information. If you put in a link back to your website, make sure that it doesn't look like your answer is spam. Provide only relevant information and you will get rewarded with high-quality traffic to your site.

10. Speed Your Site Up

Nobody likes to visit a slow website, search engines certainly don't. Make sure that your website loads up fast; here are a few tips on how to do that:

- Reduce the size of your image files.

- Use Lazy Load plugin — this cuts out unnecessary load on the server and also saves on bandwidth.

- Install Cache — this will optimize the speed of your site. I mentioned a couple of them in the Plugins section but there are many more.

- Enable zlib OR gzip compression.

- Get rid of any themes or plugins that you are not using to help speed things up and to improve on site security.

- Compress JS and CSS files together to minimize your scripts, using a plugin.

- Don't resize your images in HTML. Instead use a proper image editor or online resizing tool.

11. Install Google Analytics

And when you do, make sure that you pay proper attention to the results. It's a free tool, so you don't have any excuses! It can give you a load of information — where your traffic is coming in from, which sites are giving you the high-quality traffic, new vs. returning visitors, and much more. While most bloggers tend to think that Twitter and Facebook are the best channels for traffic to come through, it really depends on the type of website you have. By using Google Analytics, you can see at a glance which bits of your campaign are working and what needs to be improved or ditched.

Don't Give Up

You are not going to see an instant stream of traffic overnight, so give it time. Be consistent in your methods and let things build up gradually. Don't give up if you don't see a positive result immediately. It takes time to build up trust so keep on leaning and exercise patience — you will win in the end.

Chapter 9
Commonly Encountered Problems

Once you gain enough experience to work in WordPress with ease, you will want to try out different themes and customize your blog to your liking. As easy as WordPress makes customizations, there are no guarantees that WordPress will always work the way you want it to. Always remember to have a backup of your databases so that, if and when things do go haywire, all your data can be restored easily.

WordPress is extremely user-friendly, which obviously means you are going to try out different combinations of customizations and sometimes, it can crash or display error messages. When it does, do not panic, as there are over 70 million WordPress users and the chances of one among the 70 million having encountered the same problem you have is gigantic. Before taking drastic measures, do some research and find out if the same problem has been encountered by someone else and, if it has, how it was solved. Most of the time, this should solve your problem and you can have your website up and running in no time. In case it doesn't, and you are unable to find out the root cause, and no one is able to help you, it might be time for you to make use of those backups that you are recommended to have.

Most errors can be fixed by slight tweaking with the help of your FTP client. With Windows, this shouldn't be a problem, as you can use FileZilla, which is absolutely free. For a Mac, however, if you aren't comfortable with your web host's file manager and you need an FTP client, use Cyberduck to perform file transfer. It's free, and there are lots of tutorials for using it.

Here are some commonly encountered problems in WordPress:

White Screen

Infamously known as the 'White Screen of Death', this occurs when there is a database or PHP error. Do not panic when this happens, because it is a very common error and occurs to almost everyone who tries out different themes and plugins and uses up a lot of the available space.

Solutions:

Disable all your plugins first. Check your website and, if the white screen disappears, it means it's not the plugins at work. Now start activating each plugin one by one. As tedious as it may sound, this is the best way to figure out if a plugin is what caused the error. Remove this plugin, as it may not be compatible with other plugins or even your theme. Activating it again will cause the same error to occur.

Some users find that when they update their theme, the white screen appears. You want to go to your admin page, and activate the default 'Twenty Fifteen" theme to clear the white screen, and then you can activate another theme of your choice.

At times, when you use up your memory, you end up with the white screen of death. You could manually increase your limit, but if you do not know basic coding, it is better to contact your host and request them to fix this issue.

No Changes after Update

At times, your website won't show minor updates and changes that you had made previously from your admin page. This is because your cache stores website data so it can load the page faster when you visit it again. If these changes were minor, your browser would think of the change as insignificant, and will not load the new data.

Solution:

Simply clear your cache after the update, and check your website. The changes should be made, and the website will load at a slower rate than before after you clear your cache.

Sidebar Appearing Below

This is another common error experienced by many WordPress users. The sidebar gets displayed below the content instead of being at the sides. If this happened recently after installing a plugin or changing a theme, then the following solution will help:

Disable the last few plugins and activate them one by one, while constantly checking your website. If the sidebar moves to the bottom when a particular plugin is activated, remove the plugin. It's not compatible with the theme you are using.

Sometimes the theme itself may cause this error. For this, you have to check if you have every "<div>" block closed. If this doesn't solve your problem, then try changing themes.

Improper Dashboard Display

Sometimes, your dashboard stops displaying its links in the organized way it used to be. This is most likely because of your firewall and proxy (if you are using one) not allowing certain CSS files to load properly. It may also be because of outdated plugins.

Solution:

Clear your proxy and firewall cache, and try again.

Update your plugins, especially the ones related to the Dashboard.

Maintenance Error

When you update your blog with a big change, WordPress automatically pulls down the website and displays an "Under Maintenance" message whenever your website is opened. But sometimes, this page remains if the update gets corrupted or fails.

Solution:

Head to your website's root directory via FTP.

Once there, delete the file called *.maintenance*. Try refreshing your website now, and if it still displays the maintenance page, your WordPress is probably outdated - try upgrading WordPress to the latest version. This should solve the maintenance error.

Spam Posts

This is a common problem encountered by users who have a lot of traffic in their website. If you have enabled the option to let your followers post without your acceptance, you risk being spammed. Spams are annoying, and give your dedicated followers the impression that you don't really care about the comments if you don't do something about it.

Solution:

Akismet is a great spam blocker plugin, but it is not free if you own a commercial or business website. If you are a personal blogger, however, Akismet is free and recommended. It easily blocks the spam posts you would receive, saving you a mountain of trouble in deleting those posts.

You can moderate all the comments yourself, but you could easily get tired out, as the posts won't appear on your website, but you will have all the spam posts in your pending list.

Try to limit the number of hyperlinks a post can have. A common characteristic of a spam post is a ridiculous number of hyperlinks. If a post has a huge number of hyperlinks, don't allow it to be posted. You can change this from your settings in your admin page.

If you do not want to pay for a spam-blocking plugin, you can try out free plugins (though they won't be as effective), such as Simple Comments.

Pages and Posts Getting Deleted

This is a problem that people encounter only when they get a large amount of traffic on their website, and have a number of people working under them. If you suddenly wake up one morning to find a couple of your posts missing, chances are you either got hacked, or one of the people working for you deleted them.

Solutions:

The first thing you should do is check your trash. If the post or page isn't permanently deleted, you can easily bring it back from the trash, since it holds posts and pages for 30 days after deleting. If it's there, great! If it isn't, the only way to get it back would be if it were indexed by Google.

Go to your "Users" page from your Dashboard and check if there are any users there that you don't know of. If there aren't, one of your users whom you've assigned a role of Author or above is the one to blame. You can take necessary actions from here. As for your post or page, if it has been permanently deleted, there is no way to get it back, as previously stated.

Getting a Post or Page Back from Google

This is possible *only* if you had turned on the "Allow Search Engines to index this site" option, and only if your post has published for a long enough time to allow Google to cache your website. Type out the URL of the post or page in Google search, and if there's a match, hover over the double arrows to the right, and click on the "Cached" link. You can use the cached content to create a new post, and change the date to when you first published the deleted post.

In a scenario where you do not have a backup, or your post

hasn't been published long enough for Google to cache it, there is no way to get back the post or page. You will have to rewrite it from scratch once again. After this is done, make sure to add a post to apologize for what happened, as it may leave your followers wondering why the post disappeared suddenly. You can mitigate some of the damage this way, but do not expect to get a supportive and positive response from everyone. Buckle up, get ready for a lot of comments bashing you, and never repeat the same mistake of appointing someone you don't know as an editor or author again.

Chapter 10

Search Engine Optimization Tips for WordPress

In order to create a successful blog, you have to make sure that all of your content is search engine optimized. A lot of people tend to get daunted by this requirement, thinking that search engine optimization is something that can only be done by trained experts, and not the average blogger.

However, this is a complete misconception. In reality, there are several basic tips that you can use that will optimize your website or blog for search engines. This chapter features ten of the most important tips to help you accomplish this.

1. Create excellent content

Really the best way to optimize your blog for search engines is to optimize your content as well. Writing unique and high-quality content will result in your followers creating links for your blog on social media. This back-linking will be very useful when you are trying to get web crawlers to notice your blog.

If nothing else, creating unique content is the core of what allows you to keep your blog high up in search results lists. It may not be the starting point, but it helps you keep your hard-earned position.

2. Share Back links

This is a kind of "you scratch my back, I scratch yours" deal. In order to get listed by a search engine, it is essential that your blog gets detected by web crawlers. The best way for you to do this is to produce genuine, organic back links.

Remember, quality is way more important than quantity. In the end, it won't matter how many back links you have if they have been generated artificially. This is because search engines know when you are trying to get a higher rank without having earned it. This was a common problem when the Internet was still new, and search engines dealt with it fairly quickly.

In order to develop organic and natural back links, you can do a back link-sharing program with other blogs. You can create links for these blogs within your content, and these blogs can do the same for you as well. This will create back links for you, and will serve as advertising in a lot of ways.

Just make sure that you don't overdo it with the back link-sharing program. Creating back links is great, but it is not worth cluttering up your content with links to other blogs.

3. Name Your Images

A common mistake that a lot of new bloggers make with regard to search engine optimization is that they do not name their images. This is usually because they do not know that Google, and other search engines, look for images that are named, and give blogs that contain named images a lot more importance in their search engine results.

If a user is searching for a particular topic, there might be a lot of blogs with written content that pertains to their search query. However, the majority of blogs probably would not have pictures that would pertain to this search query.

Hence, by giving your images appropriate names you can get an edge over these blogs. It is an excellent way to direct traffic to your blog that would have otherwise gone to higher end blogs. Naming images is an excellent way to boost traffic and to optimize your blog for search engines.

Additionally, it is recommended that you use your image names by making them attractive and funny. Users are more likely to clink on links that lead to articles that are witty and clever.

4. Relevant and Precise Permalinks Are Key

If you want Google and other search engines to notice your blog, it is important for you to realize that your permalinks play an important role in the ranking your blog gets within a search engine results page.

Search engines generally do not count permalinks that are a random jumble of letters. They prefer permalinks that have genuine language in them, as this proves that the blog or site is genuine and provides actual content that would pertain to a user's search query.

In order to take advantage of the fact that so many bloggers do not create pertinent and relevant permalinks, it is very important that you create these permalinks for your own website. You will end up getting all of the traffic that all of the other blogs are missing out on!

In addition, search engines will probably ignore anything beyond the first four words in a permalink. Hence, you will need to make your permalinks short and precise. Keep it to four words, and try to sum up the gist of what your page has to offer by making those four words pertain to what the page is about.

5. Use Themes that Facilitate Optimization

The theme you use plays a very important role in the success of your blog. Using a cheap and lifeless theme will probably result in you losing traffic. This is due to the fact that these themes are rarely ever visually attractive and keeping things visually attractive is a key component of what makes blogs successful.

In addition, then theme you use can also end up dictating how optimized your blog will be for search engines. If you use themes that are really dense and contain a lot of code in order to make them as flashy and attractive as possible, search engine bots are going to have to crawl through this code in order to get to your content.

As a result, your content is not going to be scanned as thoroughly as it should be. You can fix this by using themes that are lighter and faster. They may end up looking not quite as good as the flashier themes, but a huge bonus is that the search engines bots will end up preferring your blog, because it will be a lot easier to sift through!

6. Use Plugins to Create Sitemaps

Google and other search engines love sitemaps. These sitemaps make it easier for the web crawlers to scan content, and ascertain whether it is pertinent to search queries or not. In essence, you are telling these web crawlers where they can find the information that they are looking for.

As a result, your blog is probably going to end up listed on Google and other search engines a lot quicker, as well. This is a huge bonus, because a lot of blogs that are news-based miss out on initial traffic, even if they blog about a topic as soon as it becomes relevant, simply because their website has not been picked up by web crawlers yet.

A lot of bloggers tend to look at the creation of a sitemap with some trepidation. After all, creating a sitemap certainly sounds like difficult work that would require a lot of coding.

This is not the case, however. Creating a sitemap is extremely easy if you use the right plugins. These plugins allow you to create a sitemap in XML format in just a few clicks, making the whole process so easy that anybody can do it!

7. Make Content that is Informative as Prominent as Possible

Bots need their jobs to be as easy as possible. This is why it is recommended that you use lighter themes in order to make it easier for them to sift through your content, as well as site maps that would make it easier for them to locate content in the first place.

Hence, it is very important that you highlight content that you feel is indicative of the feel of your blog, or the particular article that you have just written. This will make it easier for bots to see what content is supposed to be used in order to find this particular page.

Highlighting content makes it far more likely that you are going to be discovered via a search engine as well. Google will know just what sentences in you blog to look for, and if you play your cards right you should get a lot more traffic.

The key to this is to highlight sentences that people would Google. Try to include as many sentences like this as possible, but remember that it is absolutely essential that you do not overdo it. Doing too much of this would end up making your article seem like a string of keywords without any actual content, and web crawlers will begin to ignore you as a result.

8. Social Network Promotion is Essential

If you have a blog, you are probably going to have a social network as well. This includes Facebook, Twitter, and all of the other social networks that people are using these days to keep in touch.

These social networks give you access to a potentially limitless fan base. You can promote your blogs using these social networking websites and gain a lot more viewers than you would otherwise.

A great benefit of posting your blog and articles to your social networks is that it will create back links that are completely organic. If people like your content, they are likely to share it, just as people who like the content will share on their Facebook pages, as well.

It is also highly recommended that you share other people's content on your social media pages. Remember the back-scratching rule: If you create back links for people, you are going to give them a great incentive to create back links for your site as well, and this will cost you absolutely nothing.

9. Don't Try to Crack the System

If you think that you are infallible, that you can use mirror sites to generate backlinks and Google won't find out, let me just tell you that you are absolutely wrong. Google always finds out, and when it finds out it punishes the sites that were trying to be sneaky with the utmost severity.

Google takes its job very seriously. Hence, it has a lot of fail-safes in place to prevent sites from getting a search engine results rank that they do not deserve purely because of their content. Additionally, it uses a lot of techniques to ascertain whether a site has achieved a rank based on organic back links or genuine content or not.

Getting punished by Google can result in the death of your website. If you are no longer able to list your website on Google, what point is there of posting at all? No one is ever going to find your work once Google has ostracized you. If you want to get your website more hits, do it the right way. Trying to be sneaky will only result in damage to your reputation and blog.

10. Flash is the Plague

Have you ever heard the term, "avoid it like the plague"? In this situation, Flash is the plague, and you must truly avoid it as if your very life depends on it, because the life of your blog does.

It is a well-known fact that Flash is on its way out. It slows down websites enormously, it is not as efficient as some of its counterparts anymore, it is not supported by certain devices made by certain companies; and the worst thing about this utility is that it is not detected by Google.

Using Flash will only end up completely alienating your potential user base. Using WordPress code is a much better option, because Google actually detects this code, which means that your blog will have a chance of being listed in the Google search engine results.

Additionally, a large chunk of your potential user base will be viewing your website using Apple products. These products are completely incompatible with Flash, which means that all of your potential users who attempt to visit your blog from an Apple device will be completely alienated, simply because the site will not open for them.

Chapter 11
General WordPress Blogging Tips

After receiving so much specific information about WordPress, it is important that you get some general tips as well.

Be Original

It is very common for bloggers to copy what other people are doing with their blogs. But you want some attention and the best way to get attention is to do stuff that you know people are going to like. You have a unique perspective on things, and this unique perspective is fresh. It is what people will want, just have faith in yourself and go for it!

Be Truthful

Blogging is all about trust. The vast majority of blog visitors are young impressionable adults, which means that there is a lot of trust that develops between bloggers and their audience members.

If you lie, or even tweak the truth, people will stop trusting you. Your reputation will help you maintain the longevity of your blog, and nothing will harm your reputation more than lying or being dishonest in any way. Once you have lost the trust of your viewers, it is going to be a slow crawl bringing it back to what it used to be.

Be Yourself

As with all forms of entertainment and media, blogging is starting to devolve into tropes and formulaic content. This is because creating content like this is easy, and it makes it easier to attract audiences because they will be comfortable with the subject matter.

Instead of being mediocre, be awesome. Do something different. This might not get you as many hits as being one of the herd, but the audience you will create is going to be a lot more appreciative of what you do. Blogging will just be a much more fulfilling experience this way.

Be Patient

Do not expect yourself to become Studs Terkel with your very first blog post. Probably the first time you blog is going to result in content that you will be embarrassed about later on in your career. However, this content will be your starting point.

Do not get frustrated when people don't view your blog, or if you feel that you have not found your voice yet. Everything takes time, and before you know it, you will be a well-respected member of the blogging community with your own unique voice that everyone admires.

Be Thematic

It is important that you write about a certain theme in order to create an image that your readers will continue coming back for. Make it news, fashion, erotica, or anything that you feel you can write about, but at the same time it is important to realize that the content is more about quality rather than quantity.

At the end of the day, readers will be coming back for your writing style more than the general theme of your work. Once you have developed your voice, the theme will begin to matter less, but it is a good way to start off.

Be Consistent

One major problem with the way a lot of bloggers update their content is that they tend to become inconsistent in updating their blogs.

In order to maintain a loyal audience, it is absolutely essential that you update your blog in a consistent manner. This will tell your audience that you are serious about your work and that they should keep checking back to see if you have posted any new content.

Letting your blog stagnate will result in your audience disappearing because they will not feel as though you are going to uploading anything new.

Easy on the Stats Checking

A lot of bloggers tend to post something and then obsessively check the stats for it as soon as it has been posted. Your content is not going to get crazy views within the first few minutes, and checking stats obsessively will only create the illusion that your work is never going to be appreciated by anybody.

Google often takes time before listing your content, because it simply hasn't found your site yet. Hence, checking your stats too early is futile and will only demotivate you from creating new content.

Incorporate Social Media Sharing Features

The vast majority of traffic you are going to get initially is not going to be from Google, it is going to be from social media sites such as Facebook, and especially Twitter.

These social media websites are where your work absolutely must be shared during the initial stages of your blog's life. Hence, it is important that you give your viewers the option to share your posts to their social media accounts. Incorporating a plugin into your blog is a great way to do this, as it will create easy-to-use buttons.

Connect with Bloggers and Audience Members

Do not consider yourself above the rest. Other bloggers are going to be a very important part of your blogging experience. Connecting with them is a great way to get tips, to get back links and to share audience members.

In addition, it is important that you connect with audience members. By making yourself accessible to your audience members, you are going to increase your popularity. A great way to do this is to engage in question and answer sessions with your readers. This will help to forge a very personal connection with your fan base.

Get Fellow Bloggers to Guest Post

Guest posting between two bloggers that tackle similar subject matter is an excellent way for both bloggers to share their fan base, and create a mutual fan base as well.

By allowing someone to post on your blog as a guest, you are going to attract their viewers to your blog. Additionally, guest posting on someone else's blog is a great way to get their viewers to see what a great writer you are, and to subscribe to your blog to get more of you! It is part of engaging in the blogging community.

Try Not to Make Your Content Time-Specific

If you make your content specific to a certain time period, by putting time stamps on it for example, you are making it likely that it will get old and dated as time goes by.

Remember, you need to remain relevant. Try to turn your blog into a source of information rather than some kind of newspaper, even if your articles are news-based. This way people will keep coming back to look at your content long after the information within it has become old, because it will have still remained relevant.

Find a Happy Medium with Word Counts

Although there is no real science to how many words you should put into your blog post, a rule of thumb is that your post should not exceed a thousand words. Additionally, it would probably take you three hundred words to write anything of value, so this is your lower limit.

In essence, try to be succinct if you have a large topic, and expressive if you have a topic that does not have as much information to it. Find the happy medium and your audience will stay happy as well.

Don't Write for the sake of Writing

Whenever you write, whatever you are writing about needs to have a point. Audiences need to know that they are reading something of value, otherwise there is no point going to your blog at all!

If you just write random words and post it to your blog, you are going to have content but it won't be the kind of content that people would want to read. Try to focus as much as you can on content that has meaning and heart behind it, and the people who read your blog will notice and will come back for more.

Be Opinionated

A common mistake that a lot of bloggers make is that they tend to not take sides so that they are able to pander to a wider audience. This may seem like a good idea in the short run, but in the long run having strong opinions and standing by them is a great way to win respect, and a dedicated audience of people that respect you for saying what you think.

However, don't let this make you believe that you are above reproach. If you make a mistake, admit that it was a mistake and move on.

Write Succinctly

You may be tempted to write with as much descriptiveness as possible; however, this does not mean that you should write paragraphs with long sentences that never seem to end.

Sentences that drag on tend to make readers lose interest. Hence, it is very important that you craft and compose your sentences so that they don't get too long. Try to say as much as you can with as little as possible. The density of information in your sentences will turn your writing into a lush, and vivid, experience that people will keep coming back for.

Keep at It

You are a good writer, otherwise you wouldn't have the courage to take up blogging. This means that you have a chance of success. Every failure just makes it that much more likely that you are going to succeed in the future, until after a certain point you are going to be guaranteed success.

Writers and bloggers that keep at it find success; there is absolutely no doubt about that. Hence, if you keep at it and don't give in you are going to find success, and will be glad that you did not give up when the going was tough.

Write as Often as Possible

Whenever you have an idea, you should turn it into a blog post. This will turn the content of your blogs into something that is truly organic and worth coming back for.

When you have an idea, it is at its purest point in its entire life cycle. Hence, putting it onto your blog will ensure that the quality of your blog will achieve the highest standards, and that the content on your blog is purely original and written in your own voice.

Haters Mean You're Doing It Right

If someone takes the time out to badmouth what you do, you can rest assured that your work is important. If it were not important in some way nobody would find it necessary to bring you down!

Not all negative comments come from haters, however. A lot of negative comments come from people who are trying to provide constructive criticism. Try to take comments that do not include ad hominem attacks as positively as possible. They will help you to grow as a writer and improve the areas where you are lacking.

Seek Inspiration

Sometimes it is important for you to just get out there and find inspiration if it does not come to you on its own, and there are several ways in which you can do this.

One of the most important ways is to travel. Travelling allows you to meet new people, the kind of people that you might never get to meet at home. This fills up your creativity tank if you are ever in danger of running on empty.

Seeking inspiration allows you to become more accepting of the creative process, which will make you better at taking advantages of opportunities when you see them.

Differentiate Between Creation and Reaction

When you get an idea randomly without any connection to any event that you are currently experiencing, that idea is a creation. However, an idea that comes to you as a response to something you have experienced is a reaction.

Creations should be nurtured, as should reactions. However, reactions should be treated a little more carefully than creations, because they can sometimes be irrational or unintelligent in some way.

Whatever your idea is, take a step back and try to ensure that you are not reacting to anything and, if you are, that you are not reacting rashly.

Optimize for Skimmers

In today's modern age, most Internet users do not take the time to really get into any content they see on the Internet. Instead, they prefer to skim through things and see if it is worth their time before they decide to stick with it.

You should optimize your blog posts for the skimmers. Make it so that they see something interesting in the first few seconds that they skim your blog post. However, avoid sensationalism. This might attract viewers but it will prevent you from ever developing a viewer base.

Create a Mailing List

Install a call to action button in your blog and encourage people to use it in order to provide you with their email addresses. Make sure that you have asked them for permission to email regarding updates or posts to your blog, and once this permission has been gained be sure to keep them in the loop.

This way you will be able to keep the people that are truly interested up to date about the content that is available on your blog, keeping them faithful to your work.

Focus on Attractive Design

This point is very similar to the one made previously about the skimmers. If people look at a blog that is very unattractive with bold but annoying color choices, they are probably going to close your site without even taking a look at your actual content.

Hence, it is important that you invest in a blog design that is attractive. This will make people want to stay with your blog and take a look at your content. This may end up costing a little bit of money, but it will really help you to reel in your fan base.

Give Content Away

This may seem like blasphemy to you as nothing is more important than content. However, a lot of new bloggers might come up who would be starved for content. If you help these bloggers out by giving them free content, they will definitely back link to you and share your blog with their own audiences.

This will help to make you an important part of the community whilst simultaneously allowing you to grow your reader base, and keep yourself relevant. It will also boost your reputation and make you seem like a great person, which would end up making more people want to read your blog!

Ask for Expert Advice

If you see somebody who has expertise in the area of blogging, don't be afraid to ask them for a few tips. Remember, these people were in your shoes not too long ago, which means that they are probably going to understand where you are coming from.

The advice that they give is probably going to change the way you blog, so follow it to a certain degree. At the same time, if their advice does not seem compatible with your view of things, don't be afraid to ignore it.

Oftentimes, experts can be quite jaded and will not give good advice. They might be arrogant and give you petty advice. At the end of the day, you need to use your own intuition in order to ascertain whether the advice you are received is good or not.

Perhaps the best thing to do is follow what experts do rather than what they say. This will allow you to emulate the little quirks and complexities that made them successful in the first place, and will certainly make you successful as well, once you put your own spin on them.

Record Audio Versions of Your Blog Posts

We live in a world that is becoming increasingly accessible to disabled people. Nowadays, even movies come with voiceovers that are going to assist the blind by describing what is occurring in the movie to them through headphones.

This makes it possible for blind people to actively take part in content consumption, without having to worry about how they will get the gist of the content.

A lot of people are blind, and a lot of these blind people might be interested in your blog. It only makes sense that you facilitate their presence within your reader, or in this case listener, base.

Recording your blog postings can actually be really easy. If you feel as though your voice is inadequate in some way you can just have a friend read the blog posts out for you.

You can also release these audio blog posts on various entities, such as YouTube and SoundCloud, so you have a wider access to audiences. By recording your blog posts you are going to open yourself up to a whole new audience, one that will love you for including them.

Create a Catchy Title

The title of your blog will attract viewers and potential subscribers. Hence, it is obvious that the attractiveness of your title will become an important part of whether your blog post becomes successful or not.

The important thing about your title is that it also plays a role in search engine optimization. Try to make a snappy title that pertains to the content of the blog post itself but is not too long.

In addition, this title should be included in the permalink for the blog posts. You already know that permalinks cannot be longer than four words or Google will not detect them. Hence, for purposes of maintaining consistency, it is important that you at least try to ensure that the title of your blog post is four words long, or can be easily condensed into four words at the very least.

Focusing on the title may be a little frustrating, but it will really boost the chances that people will end up reading your blog post. It will also improve your chances of gaining new followers with each post.

Post Strategically

Sometimes it is important not to just post without having a plan in mind. If you have gone through a dry spell with your content, then by all means post whenever you get inspired to do. However, after a certain period, once your blog posts have become regular, it is important to start planning how you release your content.

This is because creativity tends to go dry after a certain period of time, during which time you will not post anything and your readers will end up losing faith in your blog as a result.

Try to space your blog posts out. You can also use blog posts that are tackling similar issues to create a series. This will generate long-lasting interest because your readers will be anxious to read each installment in the series.

Once the series is finished, you will find that your readers will be a lot more willing to sign up for email updates, because they will believe that your blog provides regular content that is worth checking out whenever something new has been posted. Strategic posting gains you the loyalty of your readers.

Observe Your Competitors

The world of blogging has turned into a fight for hits. There are specific numbers of users on the Internet, and we tend to forget that blogging is very similar to the world of business, in that everybody has a specific market share that they are able to exploit.

In order to get as much of a market share as possible, you have to compete with several other blogs. These blogs might have more subscribers and readers than you do. They might also be older than you are, with more experience in the field of blogging.

This makes them tough competitors, but at the same time you will be able to learn a great deal from them. If they are more successful, or more experienced than you, you should apply the techniques that they are using in your own blog.

Just try to make sure that you do not lose your own identity in the process. It is important to see what your competitors are doing, but at the same time copying them too much will lose the respect your readers have for you, and will turn you into a poor man's version of your competitor.

Keep Tabs on What's Popular

Sometimes it can be useful to see what other blogs are talking about most often. This is most useful when you are going through a creative dry spell, and need to keep the content flowing on your blog in order to keep your audience engaged.

In situations such as this, you can start posting about what is popular within the blogging community. This would keep traffic directed towards your site, and a lot of these readers might end up reading your old work. If these new readers like your old work, they might end up praising it.

Nothing stokes creativity more than appreciation. If nothing else, getting involved in popular posts will greatly boost your satisfaction rate because so many people will be visiting your site in order to check out these new posts, and some of these people will end up staying for your older stuff.

However, don't turn this into a habit. Only use this tactic to tide yourself over until your creativity comes back to you. Leaving your blog stagnant is a bad idea, as it will end up making you lose your loyal readers, and this is just a good way to keep these users engaged during your dry spell.

Check Out Google Trends

Another tactic that you can use is to check out Google trends in order to find out what people are interested in. If you need more traffic to your blog, or can't think of what to write, you can find out what is being searched on Google and write about that.

This will allow you to advertise your blog in a way, as you will be pulling in fresh traffic that might end up gaining you new readers who will stay because they like your more creative content.

Use Images

You probably know by now that creating the right visual atmosphere is a key part of keeping your potential readers engrossed in your content.

One of the best ways to catch the attention of a potential reader is to add images to your blogs. Just make sure that the images are not gratuitous, but contain colors that match the overall theme of your blog and, most important, are relevant to the blog post itself. Useless pictures are off-putting and make your readers feel betrayed. It will make people think that your blog cannot be trusted, as it does not advertise genuinely.

Be Controversial

If your views clash with the views of regular people, do not be afraid to put them out there. Even people that do not agree with your views might end up sharing your blog posts because they will find them controversial or offensive in some way.

However, be wary of being controversial for the sake of creating controversy. Often it can harm your reputation to just say things that are controversial because you want to expand your viewer base. Try to make it as natural as possible and people will appreciate it.

Ask Your Audience What It Wants

If you feel creatively dry, you can always ask your readers what they want you to write about. They will always be willing to give you advice and the bonus is that you will certainly be writing something that your readers would enjoy.

Use this as a way to solidify the faithfulness of your reader base. You can also use this technique to determine whether the content you are creating is in line with what your readers want or not, which can be particularly useful if you are planning on changing the content of your blog.

Conclusion

So now you're ready to get started. You know what it takes to really make the most of WordPress as a website, and you also know everything necessary for getting started as a blogger. Before you know it you're going to be really using this site to the best possible advantage, and you're going to be improving your own website, your blog and your reader's lives at the same time. It's all about developing yourself and constantly developing your website. Just take a little time and you'll be there before you know it.

Hopefully this book has given you what you need to not only get started, but really get moving as well. Just take the time to implement what we've talked about. There's plenty more that your WordPress website is going to have to offer you. For now, however, this is going to get you moving, and it's going to make sure that you start getting your information out there (and maybe even making some money while you're at it). WordPress can be fun and it will definitely be a great skill to develop for your future. You never know when website building as a skill may come in handy.